Bear Necessities

Mandy Shaw

Bear Necessities

Mandy Shaw

T R A P L E T
P U B L I C A T I O N S

Craftworld Series

First published in 2002 by
Traplet Publications Limited
Traplet House, Severn Drive, Upton upon Severn,
Worcestershire WR8 0JL

Publisher: Tony Stephenson

Photographs © Marie Stone, or Lynsey Piff for Traplet, as credited
Front cover photographs by Lynsey Piff; back cover photograph by Marie Stone
All illustrations by Gail Lawther, © Traplet Publications
Studio scans and pre-press work by Neil Blowers

ISBN 1 900371 85 5
British Library Cataloguing in Publication Data
A catalogue record for this book is available from the British Library

Designed and edited by Teamwork, Christopher and Gail Lawther,
44 Rectory Walk, Sompting, Lancing, West Sussex BN15 0DU

Set in Schneidler Mediaeval & *Amalthea, Van Dijk,* and Cronos Pro fonts

Printed by Stephens & George
Goat Mill Road, Dowlais, Merthyr Tydfil CF48 3TD

CONTENTS

PHOTO: LYNSEY PIFF

PHOTO: MARIE STONE

THE TEDDY BEAR is 100 years old this year, which makes this a perfect time to introduce the timeless skill of bear-making to a new generation of stitchers. In the pages of **Bear Necessities** you'll find all the information you need to begin bear-making, with patterns for bears of all shapes, sizes and fabrics, plus essential accessories such as clothes, bed quilts, and bear-centred wall-hangings. I've included a short history of the teddy bear, a story about a bear, and even a gallery for you to paste in pictures of your first bear creations! All in all, this book is a celebration of the teddy bear's life so far, and its timeless popularity.

Mandy

A brief history of the teddy bear

 The roots of the teddy bear's history lie in both German and American history, and as neither side is willing to give up first place, we must assume that the timing was concurrent.

The American story goes like this. The 26th president of the United States, Theodore ('Teddy') Roosevelt, was on a bear hunt in Mississippi. The president had no luck finding a wild bear that day, and his only chance of a kill was a bear tied to a tree by one of his entourage. He refused to kill it, and the incident was illustrated in *The Washington Post* by the political cartoonist Clifford K Berryman. Cartoons were a very important type of communication at that time, and Berryman used the bear to symbolise the president.

Very soon afterwards, the bear was made into a toy by the Michtoms, small-scale toy makers. They later went on to found the Ideal Toy Corporation, which became at one stage the largest bear-making factory in the United States. One thing that is certain is that the name teddy was taken from the President. Mind you, we also had our own Teddy, King Edward VII; I'd like to think we perhaps had some connection.

Meanwhile in Germany, a young woman whose name was Margaret Steiff set up a mail order company making soft toys. She had been confined to a wheelchair since contracting polio as a young child. She designed and made soft toys based on lifelike drawings made by her nephew, Richard, at Stuttgart Zoo. She attempted to sell these bears, called Friend Petz, at Leipzig Fair in 1903; no-one showed any interest until the close of the fair, when an American put in an order for an astonishing 3,000. The rest is history; the firm of Steiff went on to become very large.

We Brits do have a part to play in the bear's history. We exported much of the Yorkshire mohair to Germany; we also exploited the ban on German imports during both world wars and established our own soft toy industry, and have continued to make wonderful bears. Chad Valley, Merrythought, Pedigree and Deans are names to look out for.

100 years later the teddy bear is still one of our favourite soft toys; he appeals internationally to both sexes and all ages. The teddy bear appears in comics, books, magazines, cartoons, films; we see teds as television characters and mascots, and in museums and on fashion items – the list goes on and on. In fact with bear collecting (or *arctophily* as it's properly known, which means bear love) becoming so popular, we can only assume that the extraordinary success of the teddy bear will last well into the next century.

Let me introduce myself ...

I would describe myself as a maker of all things lovely – especially my four children. I've been sewing all my life; my earliest sewing memory is of a dress I made at the age of six. I created it out of a flannelette sheet, with two holes in it for my arms, and big black coat buttons holding the front together. I felt like a princess.

I have many memories of my mum at the table, sewing. I used to count the buttons and play with the pins, things my children do today. She made endless numbers of soft toys for the school fete, and I was always so proud to take them in to my teacher.

One vivid memory is when a friend of my mum's came to the door with two old teddy bears her children had grown out of, for my brother and me. I instantly fell in love with Daniel and grabbed him first. I was then plagued with guilt when Rupert, my brother's bear, was left alone and ignored. When my parents parted Daniel and Rupert came with us to our new home. They were by then very worn and minus a limb or two; the wood fill in their faces had disintegrated, and they began to look even sadder than before. My mother offered to re-stuff and repair them: I was horrified – it would be like giving them a face-lift and distorting their features.

Imagine what they look like now, nearly forty years later. I looked for a sign of a button in the ear, indicating a rare Steiff bear, but to no avail. Instead,

Me with my much-loved and worn old friends Rupert and Daniel (Daniel's the one in the dress!)

while researching them in a book, I discovered that they were bought in a Woolworth's store in England before World War II, and that they were made from low-quality plush, typical of the cheaper range of bears at the time. Nevertheless, I still love them badly, and since my brother died as a young man, Rupert is all I have from his childhood.

I followed in my mother's footsteps and have been sewing ever since, especially making dolls, quilts, and teds. My husband and I married young, and we've spent hours and hours doing up our lovely Edwardian homes. Phil is the most amazing joiner; he made virtually everything.

Just imagine my fun when three beautiful daughters came along (not all together!); it was like re-living my childhood all over again. I made them so many clothes it was ridiculous. I was even known to wake them late in the evening to try on my new creations. Our little boy came along later; at last a carpenter's mate. I loved birthdays, party games, cake-making, decorating the house and – best of all

– present making. We always made our children's presents; they were festooned with dolls' houses, rocking horses, mini Welsh dressers, shops, work-benches, Noah's arks, dolls; and, of course, teds. They all have a growing collection as they reach many milestones in their lives. I've just made a miniature bear for my eldest daughter's 18th.

Once the girls were at school, I worked part-time in a patchwork shop, Country Crafts. I started teaching there and at Adult Education centres, and haven't looked back since. We've had some exciting times, such as when a homes magazine did an article on us. A camera crew came and took over the house (which, incidentally, took two weeks to spring clean! I have my talents, but cleaning is not one of them). The results were lovely, and it was only when I saw our home in the magazine, that I realised we had created something really special.

My children with their growing collection of teds. From left to right: Abbie, Jess, Harvey and Harriet (Alfie's sneaked into the photograph as well, I notice ...)

Six months later a local television company, who had seen the magazine, contacted me asking to do a slot on a programme called *At Home* with Maggie Philbin. I had to design a beach bag. I only shared my dressing room with Danny La Rue! Beggars can't be choosers; if I had been there the previous week it would have been Adam Faith ... Another six months later I was at Elstree studio talking about my quilts on *Leisure Hour* – this time nine months pregnant and not so glamorous. Someone described me as looking like a cottage loaf!

And now here I am fulfilling another ambition: writing a book about another love in my life, bears. I hope you find my patterns easy to use and find a creative streak in you that you can nurture and develop to give you so much pleasure. Some people come to my workshops thinking 'I can't do this', 'that's not right,' 'I'm no good at this'; but when they go home they're so pleased with the ted they've made, warts and all, that they radiate

confidence. Surely that's all worth it. I still get a buzz from creating a new character. And when my husband says 'what's that smug smile about?', I think 'silly man, he should recognise that smile by now – I've made something new again!'

I recognise that smile in my children and have always encouraged them to be 'makers'; it doesn't take any money, just a little time. Time is so precious when you are a child, and it goes all too quickly. Turn that telly off, forget the washing up, get the sewing stuff out, sit the children around a table, and make Simple Simon (see page 11). For me, life doesn't get much better!

> ### *A loving stitch*
> ### *a nurtured seam*
> ### *to fulfil a childhood dream.*
>
> *A little ditty sent to me by my Uncle Steve when he knew I was writing a book.*

Simple Bears

The bears in this chapter are all very quick and easy to sew; I've included this section in the book as a little light relief – not because I don't think you're capable of making a mohair bear straight away! You'll also find that you can readily adapt and customise these bears using different fabrics and trimmings, enabling you to design your own ted. No two bears are ever alike, especially if you use different fabrics; they can miraculously get thinner and fatter with no effort from you (sounds familiar ...)

Simple Simon

♥ **MATERIALS** ♥

14 x 9in (36 x 23cm) piece of felt

matching sewing thread

a handful of stuffing

two black beads for eyes

black thread for nose

soft pencil

thin card, eg from a cereal packet

A big 'thanks' to my friend Jo, who gave me this pattern; she uses it a lot with a play-scheme she helps run. I have given the design a little nip and tuck, and it's now ready for you to use with your children, grandchildren, or friend's children. This is the simplest bear you could hope for, so if you're completely new to bear-making, try this one first.

In our busy lives today we don't spend enough time sitting down with children teaching them craft skills. Creating things makes our children feel so important, pleased with themselves and confident. My poor children groan when their friends come round to play and they want to sew. I remember once when we were all sitting round a table and a child took a needle from the pincushion to thread; she was struggling, and when I went to help, I realised why – it was a pin that she had in her hand, not a needle! She was thirteen, and had never learned the difference.

Talking of needles: be prepared to re-thread it a thousand times, and make sure you have some decent sewing needles. I went to help out in a classroom once and found the children sewing with blunt tapestry needles – no wonder they're put off sewing.

This bear can be sewn by hand or by machine. Children are fine with machines as long as they are supervised, and taught to keep their hands away from the needle. Teach them to go around the ears slowly, stopping and starting as necessary; the sewing line will then be smoother.

Time and time again when I'm teaching adult workshops, I hear students saying that when they were children they were made to unpick and redo their stitching until it was perfect. I think this is so demoralising; if the child or student is happy with the finished result, then that's all that matters. My daughter, who was nine at the time, made a quilt for an exhibition; she was tired and put the binding on a little skewiff. I gently suggested she might need a little help to correct it; she said no, and went on to win the championships for the under 16s!

♥ INSTRUCTIONS ♥

1 Trace or photocopy the template on page 58 and stick the pattern sheet to the card. Cut out the bear shape.

2 Fold the felt in half. Lay the template on the felt and, in pencil, trace around the bear shape onto it.

3 Pin the two layers of felt together. **Don't cut the shape out**; it's much easier, especially for children, if you sew on the marked lines and cut out afterwards.

4 Sew on the pencil line with a running stitch, backstitch, or by machine. Remember to leave the gap for stuffing.

5 Carefully cut out the teddy shape, making a little snip under his arms and between his legs.

6 Turn the bear shape the right way out.

7 Stuff the bear and sew up the side opening.

8 Sew on two beads for eyes, and use the black thread to embroider a nose.

Jonnie Bear

Jonnie is a simple folk bear with no joints; he's nice and easy to make while you're waiting for that mohair to arrive in the post! Make him in denim, fleece, calico, kunin felt or plush, in fact any light- to medium-weight fabric. The type of fabric you use will determine the look and the size of your finished bear, as you can see from the two above; they were both made from the same pattern. A fabric such as fleece will stretch and make a chubbier ted; denim, calico and cotton have less 'give', and produce a leaner body. (Why do I always design my teds with big tummies and feet? You know what they say about dogs looking like their owners ... is there no hope for me?)

♥ INSTRUCTIONS ♥

1 Trace or photocopy the templates on pages 59-61: glue the pattern sheets on thin card, and cut out the pattern pieces.

2 Mark the pattern onto the wrong side of the fabric, and cut out the pieces.

3 Sew the two legs, remembering to leave them open at the top and also to leave a gap in the back as indicated on the pattern. Trim the seams, and turn the right way out.

4 Sew the legs onto the bottom of the back (**a**), in the position indicated on the pattern. (Remember that the feet should be facing inwards.)

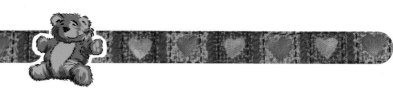

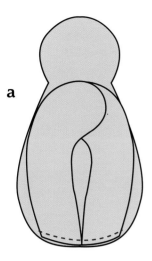

a

5 With the right sides together, sew the two body pieces between the points marked A and B. Open out the body and pin the back piece to it, tucking the legs into the body away from any seams. Sew all the way around, leaving the bottom open.

6 Trim the seams and snip carefully under the chin; turn the right way out. The legs should be dangling from the front of the body.

7 Sew both arms, remembering to leave a gap at the back for stuffing.

8 Firmly stuff the head and body, and close the bottom opening with ladder stitch (see page 33). This sometimes seems difficult because of the chubby tummy, but if you use ladder stitch you can slightly gather the tummy side to fit the back. If only life was that easy!

9 Pour some pellets into the feet up to the ankle; softly stuff the rest of the legs and close the openings with ladder stitch

10 Pour some pellets into the arms up to the wrist, and softly stuff the rest of the arm pieces. Close the openings with ladder stitch.

11 Attach the arms using extra-strong thread and two buttons; sew right through the body using a long needle.

12 Stitch the ear sections together in pairs, right sides together, leaving the lower edges open. Turn the pieces right side out, then attach them using the method shown on page 33.

13 Embroider the nose using six strands of embroidery thread. Attach the eyes in the positions indicated on the pattern, using the extra-strong thread. Add a button to the bear's ear.

♥ MATERIALS ♥

24 x 18in (61 x 45cm) rectangle of your chosen fabric

one bag of polyester stuffing

1oz/100g of plastic pellets (optional)

two 8mm black buttons, boot buttons or plastic eyes

two buttons about the size of a penny, for joining on the arms

black embroidery thread

long needle

12 x 9in (30 x 21cm) felt for the waistcoat

contrasting embroidery thread for the blanket stitch

two small buttons or poppers for the waistcoat

PHOTO: MARIE STONE

To make the waistcoat

1 Trace or photocopy the waistcoat pattern pieces on page 62 and cut them from thin card. Use them as templates to cut the pattern pieces out of felt.

2 With right sides together, sew the shoulder seam and the side seams.

3 Decorate the raw edge with a blanket stitch all the way around.

4 Use blanket stitch to attach the two pockets, then add two buttons or poppers.

Tweeny Beanie Bears
TASJ, GEORGIE AND JACK

Whenever I make a small bear the word 'fiddly' crops up in my head. These three may well be slightly fiddly, but they are very cute, cheap to make, reasonably quick, and extremely popular with all ages. My teenage daughters' boyfriends all wanted one when they saw them lined up on the table. And I've just made a pair for a wedding I'm going to; instead of the customary wooden spoon, I'll give them the bears, one dressed in a tutu and the other in a waistcoat. Ah – sweet!

♥ INSTRUCTIONS ♥

1 Trace or photocopy the pattern pieces on page 63 and stick them onto the card; cut them out. Fold the piece of fabric in half, right sides together, and use the templates as a guide for cutting out the fabric pieces (**a**). (If you're using scraps of fabric rather than one large piece, make sure that you cut one pattern in reverse each time, otherwise you'll end up making far more teds than you intended to ...)

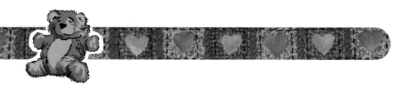

2 Put the front pieces right sides together, pin them well, and sew from point A to point B (**b**). You need to sew an ⅛in (2mm) seam and use a very small stitch; because of the very small seam allowance, sew all seams twice. Snip under the chin where indicated.

3 Repeat the process using the back pieces, sewing from C to D, and remembering to leave an opening in the back for turning and stuffing (**c**).

4 Open out the front and back sections; with right sides together, pin the two body parts together all the way around, matching ears, legs and arms carefully; stitch (**d**).

5 Very carefully snip under the arms, neck and crotch.

6 Turn the bear the right way out. I find it easier to turn small parts by pushing a small, blunt-ended pair of scissors into the end of the hand or foot and rolling the fabric over the scissors.

7 Stuff the head, paying particular attention to the nose. It's best to put very small individual balls into the nose – otherwise, for some strange reason, the stuffing just tends to come out and you have an unstuffed nose.

8 Pop your ted into the bag of pellets and fill him up from in there – otherwise you get pellets all over the place. Give him a good shake so that the pellets get to the bottom of his hands and feet, then ladder stitch up the back opening.

♥ **MATERIALS** ♥

lightweight fabric (don't even attempt to make these little bears out of thick denim, it's nigh on impossible)

matching sewing thread

two black beads for the eyes of each bear

black embroidery thread for the noses

half a cup of plastic pellets or pre-baked lentils for each bear

a small amount of stuffing

thin card (from a cereal packet or similar)

3 x 9in (7.5 x 21cm) cotton or similar fabric for each skirt

9 Sew a small button in his ear (I used one I pinched from a Barbie jacket).

10 Sew on the two beads for eyes, and embroider a nose using two strands of embroidery thread. See page 33 for ideas on varying the expressions of the different bears.

11 The skirts are made in the same way as the clothes for the larger teds (instructions for these are on pages 37-38).

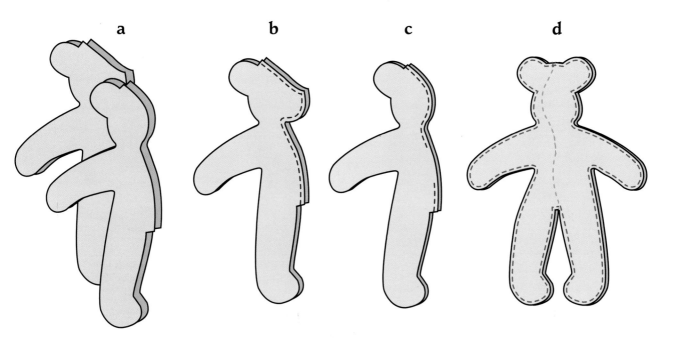

a   b   c   d

Mohair Bears

This is the chapter where I share with you everything I've ever learned about making mohair bears, from the cutting of the mohair down to the smallest detail of sewing on a nose. My intention is that you'll make a bear that will last a lifetime, become worn and loved, and won't go through the humiliation suffered by poor old Rupert and Daniel (see page 8 – their body parts have let them down because they were made of low-quality artificial silk plush). Every person I know who has made a bear using one of these patterns has been very pleased with herself and the finished ted. So, find (no – make) the time to create a bear, and enjoy!

Materials and Equipment

✪ Materials ✪

There are various different materials that you need for making and stuffing a bear; some of these are readily available in craft shops, and the others can be bought from the specialist suppliers listed on page 56.

♥ MOHAIR FUR ♥

This is manufactured from the coats of angora goats; the fibres are collected and then woven onto a cotton backing. Mohair is only manufactured in Yorkshire and Germany. German Schulte mohair is the best quality in the world – it's made specifically for the teddy bear market, and has been for a century; it's the fur that is used for the famous Steiff bears.

There is absolutely no doubt in my mind that this type of fur makes the best bears. I've tried synthetic furs, and even though there are some very good ones on the market, they don't age or wear as well. Mohair comes in different types: short, medium, curly, and distressed; it has a luxurious feel, and makes the bears look and feel like old ones. I like the distressed mohairs best; they give the bears great age straight away. Mohair is expensive, but bears made out of this will last a lifetime. Fortunately I've found some very good suppliers (see page 56). Don't be daunted by the price per metre: the mohair is wide, and you only need an 8in (20cm) strip for some of my patterns.

♥ ALTERNATIVES TO MOHAIR ♥

Now if you really can't wait to get some mohair you could be really trendy and start recycling fabric from home. Denim is a favourite of mine, the more faded the better, and it makes a wonderful ted. If you don't have any at home, go to a charity shop and buy an old shirt or skirt; that will be enough to make a soft, medium-sized ted; jeans will make a firmer one. Don't bother using joints in the bears, except for the head; put the arms and legs on with great big buttons. Velvet is also very good.

PHOTO: MARIE STONE

If you're feeling very creative, find an old wool blanket, cut it into four, and dye one quarter with a machine dye – any colour you like. Just follow the instructions on the packet; it really is very easy. This makes a very different, individual bear, just as loveable as the furry kind. If you're keen on embroidery you could embellish the bear with stitches using silk ribbons and unusual threads – perhaps even some buttons, like crazy patchwork. Goodness, I'm getting carried away now ... Calico is another option for bear-making. I've even seen a calico bear given as a present at a party; everyone signed their name on the bear using a permanent pen. What a lovely idea for a gift.

I know you're waiting for me to mention synthetic fur: sorry, I can't go there, but there are a couple of lovely products that you can buy in good craft shops and suppliers, and they are kunin shaggy felt and kunin plush felt. The shaggy one is slightly distressed. These felts cut and sew easily without fraying; they are soft and fluffy, and get even softer when washed. There; what a choice of different materials. No excuses now.

♥ PAW AND PAD FABRIC ♥

The felt that you can buy in craft shops isn't suitable for making paws and pads; it's too flimsy and weak. Soft leather is lovely, as are moleskin, velvet and really thick wool felt. You may be able to recycle some of these fabrics from garments you have at home, but if not, you can buy an excellent suedette from the same supplier as the fur.

♥ STUFFING ♥

Polyester and other artificial fibres are the stuffings most commonly used today, because of their cleanliness and low flammability. This is one material where I actually prefer not to buy the best quality, as it's very soft and springy and won't always stay in place – a medium-quality stuffing works best. In the olden days they used wood shavings to stuff soft toys; as a child investigating a small hole in my ted I discovered this for myself ...

♥ PLASTIC PELLETS ♥

I love these, and put them in almost all my bears (only in the tummy, hands and feet, though – otherwise they become far too heavy and look severely depressed). They give a lovely weighty, squidgy feel to bears. You can use lentils or rice, but these must be baked dry in a very hot oven to kill any mites they may have on them. I have had a nasty experience of a ted growing little animals – very unpleasant!

✪ Tools ✪

Most of the tools you'll need for bear-making can be found in the average home.

Stuffing tool

This can be as sophisticated as the handle on your wooden spoon, or, if you're careful, a large pair of blunt-ended scissors (used closed). Chopsticks work well for the smaller teds.

Scissors

You'll need paper scissors for cutting out the card templates, plus small sharp-pointed scissors (embroidery ones are ideal).

Awl

This tool has a sharp metal spike, which is great for making holes in the fur for joints and eyes. Have a good rummage in your toolbox or your husband's shed and you may find one, but if not, embroidery scissors will do.

Pencil

A sharp soft pencil is good for marking the patterns onto the fur; if the backing of your fur is dark, use a black biro, or tailor's chalk.

Glue stick

Handy for glueing templates onto card.

Thin card

I've found that it's much easier to make a cardboard template to trace round onto the mohair than to try and use a paper pattern; I stick the paper template onto the thin card from cereal packets and then cut round the lines. This way the pattern doesn't lose its shape and is easier to store, especially if you punch a hole in each pattern piece and tie them all together when you've finished.

Wire brush

A suede shoe brush (a new one of course, unless you're planning for a really distressed look) is ideal for brushing the pile out of the seams when the bear is finished; alternatively, you can buy wire brushes from the suppliers on page 56.

✪ Extras ✪

You'll find the following items useful additions to your basic sewing kit.

Sewing threads

Use a good brand of ordinary sewing thread, 100% cotton, and match it to the back of the mohair. You will also need some extra-strong thread, such as buttonhole thread, to sew up the head, seams and eyes. Fine, strong fishing line is great for attaching eyes.

Perlé cotton, coton à broder and stranded embroidery floss are all suitable threads for embroidering the nose and other features.

❊ *HANDY HINT* ❊

Don't use old cottons that have been exposed to sunlight; they deteriorate. Many people come along to classes with their granny's extra-strong thread, that's the best part of 100 years old, but it's not worth using; all threads deteriorate when they're exposed to light for a long period of time.

Growler

These are available from good craft shops and suppliers, and come in two sizes: medium and large. Be warned, they do sound like cows and sheep, but once buried in the bear they make a more realistic bear sound (whatever that is!) I don't use growlers on the smaller teds, such as Rosie and Blanche, because I like their tummies to be soft and cuddly; it's easier to hide a growler among the stuffing in larger bears such as Jodie and Charlie.

Eyes

I like my bears best with black boot-button eyes. If you look through your granny's (or great granny's) button tin you may find a pair of original boot buttons which would be lovely, but if not you can get them through craft suppliers; these eyes will be made of glass and have a little twinkle.

Please note that if the bear is for a young child you should use plastic safety eyes (above).

Funnel

A funnel helps to get the plastic pellets into the bear and not on the floor.

Needles

As well as your usual needles, you will need a 3in or 5in needle; these longer ones make sewing on the eyes much easier.

Thimble

If you're used to using a thimble, you'll find it invaluable when you're sewing on the eyes. If not, get the plasters ready! (Did you know that spit is the best stain-removal agent for blood on fabric? It contains a special enzyme that seems to neutralise the blood.)

Glass-headed pins

These are an important item, as the mohair will need to be pinned well to prevent it sliding around. The glass heads of the pins will show you where they are among all the fur and prevent you leaving them in and causing accidents. I once found a needle and thread in my mashed potato. And another in the bottom of the freezer!

Pearl button

This is something I put on all my teds – in the ear of course – to identify them as mine. I try and recycle buttons from my children's clothing; have a look on unwanted garments, and you'll probably find an assortment of buttons in different sizes, like the ones on the right.

Joints

Plastic safety joints are quick and easy to use, especially when you're making your first bear. There are the purists out there who only use the wooden joints with washers; you often need special tools to assemble these, and as the fur is expensive, I don't want you dashing out buying extras that aren't necessary. The advantage of the hardboard joints is that you can get a tighter fit; it's worth experimenting with these when you are more experienced.

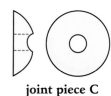

joint piece A   joint piece b   joint piece C

Sewing machine

A well-loved, oiled, and de-fluffed machine is all you need: no fancy gadgets. I use a fifty-year-old Singer Featherweight. But the most important thing for your sanity, and that of your family, is that it hasn't been stuck in the cupboard disused for years, with you expecting it to sew perfectly right away. Give it some tender loving care, a drop of oil, a good clean, and a new needle (Jeans size 14 or 16, depending on the thickness of your fur; these are wonderfully sharp needles and sew through anything).

Check that you've threaded the machine up correctly, and that the bobbin is in the right way and evenly wound. These are common errors that make sewing machine repair-men very rich. Do all this and your machine should perform for you beautifully.

If you have a ¼in foot for your machine this will be an excellent guide for your seams; if not, the ordinary straight sewing foot will be fine.

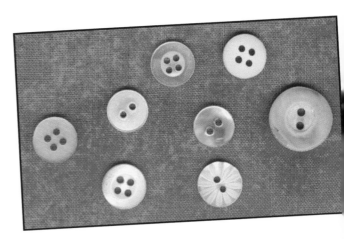

Now you've warmed up with a couple of easy bears, it's time to introduce the furry family. I make no apologies for my collection of bears being worn and slightly scruffy; they've all been made as gifts for my family and friends to celebrate special occasions, and are much adored, loved and played with. I far prefer a bear whose nose has had too much loving to one that has faded and collected dust on a shelf. There are no more beautiful sights than seeing my four-year-old son walking up the garden path with Charlie under one arm being lovingly wrestled – or waving my daughter off to Brownie camp with Jodie (in her Brownie uniform of course) strapped into a car-seat next to her. These memories are what childhoods are made of.

Jodie

A large, 20in (50cm) tall bear *(top right)* with traditional long arms and big feet (strange that we all have big feet in our family). She has a big round tummy, a warm loving face and big eyes, and because she's stuffed with pellets she's very heavy. Her size works to her advantage because she fits into baby clothes. I've used an expensive, dense, long-pile, slightly curly fur, which gives her great hugability; even so, she still worked out a quarter of the price of a famous branded variety, and she's got lots more character.

Charlie

Charlie *(right)* is a medium-sized bear measuring in at 15in (38cm); he has some pellets in his body but is not too heavy. Charlie's body is slightly under-stuffed, which makes him nice and squashy. He's a good-sized bear who makes a good first project if you're new to bear-making. I used a sparse, long-length pile fur, which gives him a very mischievous and naughty look. I have, however, seen him made in all sorts of colours and lengths of fur, and I'm always impressed with the outcome. Don't forget: a nip and a tuck turns him into a girl bear!

PHOTOS: LYNSEY PIFF

Rosie

A bear with a little bit of attitude. For a start she's thinner, 12in (30cm) tall, has no pouchy tummy, and has more defined features *(right)*. She looks like a traditional bear with her long, slim arms and legs. I made her in a very sparse fur, but if you use a fuller one she appears plumper. Because of her thin arms and legs you have to be especially careful when sewing your seams, otherwise when you stuff her you might tear them. She is, though, quite quick to make and considerably cheaper than Jodie, especially if you use the cheap fur.

Blanche

Blanche Lydia to be precise *(below, right)*. Named after a ward, and made for my daughter while she was in hospital, Blanche even has a scar on her tummy to match. She looks like the youngest of the bunch and is not endowed with natural good looks. Her charm, however, is in her slightly hunched shoulders, small eyes, thick thighs and big feet! She has a wonderful collection of clothes that I made while sitting by Harriet's side for days; a very special teddy. The fur I used had one of those piles that went everywhere; I wasn't at all sure of its direction, but she still looked good.

✪ Requirements ✪

On pages 28-35 you'll find general instructions for assembling the bears; these are virtually identical for each member of the family, but because the bears are different sizes you need different amounts of materials for each one. I've listed their requirements opposite, along with a diagram (see page 26) for laying out the pattern pieces on the mohair – this arrangement should help ensure that you have all the pattern pieces the right way round on the pile, and will help you to make best use of the fur.

PHOTOS: LYNSEY PIFF

JODIE

♥ MATERIALS ♥

20in (50cm) mohair fur
(she will look great in any quality and thickness)

10in (25cm) square of suedette

four bags of stuffing, medium quality

2lb plastic pellets

skein of black embroidery thread

extra-strong thread

cotton to match the back
of the fur

two 15mm plain black eyes

five 65mm plastic joints

long (5in/13cm) needle

large growler

CHARLIE

♥ MATERIALS ♥

10in (25cm) mohair fur

8in (20cm) square of suedette

two bags of stuffing

8oz plastic pellets

small growler

five 45mm safety joints

extra-strong thread

skein of black embroidery thread

cotton to match the back of the fur

two 10mm plain black eyes

BLANCHE

♥ MATERIALS ♥

8in (20cm) fine or sparse fur
(a really thick fur will bulk her out too much)

5in (13cm) square of suedette

cotton to match the back
of the fur

two 5mm plain black eyes

five 30mm plastic joints

one bag of stuffing

6oz plastic pellets

black embroidery thread

ROSIE

♥ MATERIALS ♥

8in (20cm) mohair fur;
fine or sparse quality
(a really thick one will be much more difficult to sew)

5in (13cm) square of suedette

cotton to match the back of the fur

two 8mm plain black eyes

five 30mm plastic joints

one bag of polyester stuffing

4oz plastic pellets

black embroidery thread

Getting Ready to Stitch

✪ Preparing the Pattern ✪

The first stage of making a bear involves preparing the pattern. If you take time making a good-quality copy of the pattern, and are precise in marking, pinning and stitching, you should be rewarded with a beautiful bear.

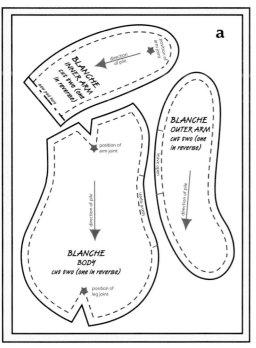

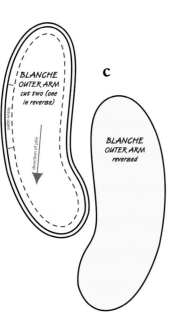

♥ INSTRUCTIONS ♥

1 Check the pattern pieces in the book carefully and make sure that you're familiar with all the bits that you need for the bear you're making. You'll find that each pattern piece is clearly marked with the bear's name, and instructions on whether you need to cut one or more pieces from the fabric.

2 Trace or photocopy the relevant pattern pieces onto good-quality white paper. Glue each whole sheet onto the front of a disused cereal packet (**a**) and cut out the template(s), this will save you cutting out the pattern pieces twice, and give you a firm template (**b**) to mark round onto the fur.

3 Remember to make two templates, using one the other way around, when the pattern says 'cut one in reverse' (**c**).

4 Make holes through the card where the joints are marked (**d**).

5 Punch holes in all the pattern pieces, so that they're ready to be tied together with a piece of ribbon when you've finished with them (**e**). This keeps the pattern pieces together and in good order.

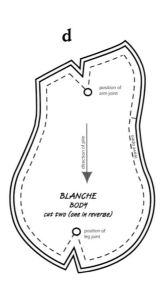

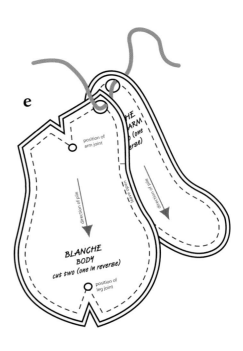

✪ *Marking out the Pattern* ✪

This is where many people start sweating. You've spent a lot of money on your mohair and things could go horribly wrong from here. Be reassured, though; if you take your time, and are nice and accurate, a beautiful bear is about to be born. Put the video on for the kids, send your husband out to his shed, make a coffee, take a deep breath and let's start.

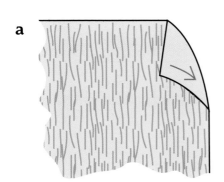

a

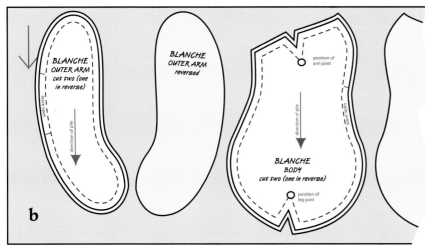

b

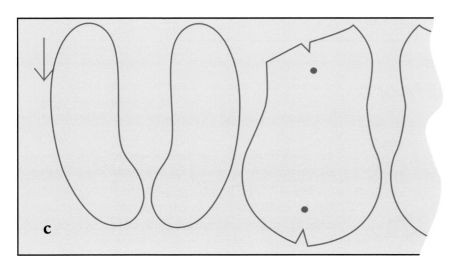

c

♥ INSTRUCTIONS ♥

1 Most importantly you need to establish the direction of your mohair. This varies in all furs. Lay the fabric onto the table with the furry side (also known as the pile) facing you; now give it a stroke as if it was a friendly old cat. Start from the top of the fabric and stroke it down towards you. If the fur is smooth and not ruffled you have it in the right direction; if it's rough and ruffled, turn it round until you find the smooth stroke.

This sounds extremely straightforward, but in some fur, especially the short type, the 'grain' seems to go in all directions. Look carefully at the fur; find the direction in which most hair seems to lie and take that as the smooth stroke. If you come across a fur that's particularly confusing, don't worry too much; as Delia (one of our UK television chefs) says, 'anything made out of something so good will still taste lovely'!

2 Now that you've found the direction of the pile, you need to mark it (**a**). Turn a corner of the fabric over to the wrong side and use biro to draw an arrow on the selvedge indicating the direction of the pile.

3 Turn the mohair over so that the wrong side of the fabric is now facing you.

4 All the information that you'll need for cutting is marked on the pattern pieces, so look at them carefully. Each individual teddy pattern in the book has its own layout for how to arrange the pieces on the fabric. The pattern pieces fit snugly together to avoid wastage (**b**); this means that sometimes the pattern pieces will actually touch each other.

5 Using a pencil, biro or tailor's chalk, trace round all the pattern pieces on the wrong side of the fabric, matching the arrow directions on the pattern with the marking you made in the selvedge (**c**). Remember that the paws and pads are cut out of suedette.

cutting layout for Charlie

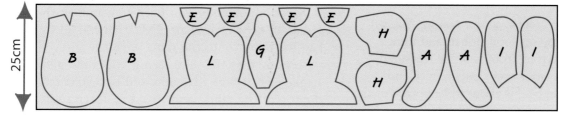

cutting layout for Rosie

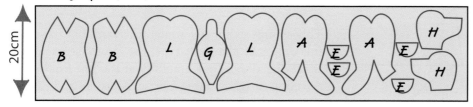

cutting layout for Blanche

KEY

A arm
B body
E ear
G gusset
H head
I inner arm
L leg

cutting layout for Jodie

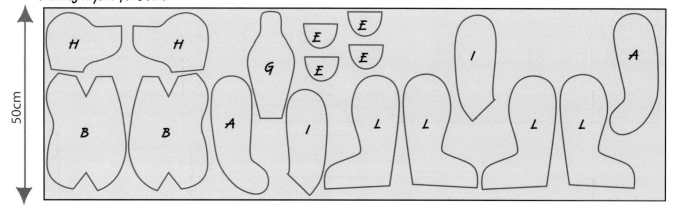

✪ *Cutting out the Pattern* ✪

Now it gets exciting: you're going to cut out all the pieces. There is, though, a special way of cutting to prevent harsh and straight-cut seams (which come out a bit like a bad hairdo), so 'do as you would be done unto' and take a bit of extra time and care here!

You need to cut only the backing fabric of the material, never the pile. To do this you'll use small, sharp-pointed scissors; slide the points of your scissors under the pile and take small snips (*right*), not large snaps like a crocodile. To remember this I tell people to say 'snip snip, not snap snap', and in my workshops you can hear a whole batch of people saying this under their breath when they're cutting out! The longer the pile, the more important this is, so that the fur is left to cover and partially hide the seams, and soften their effect.

Don't cut out anything until you've marked all the pattern pieces onto your fabric, and double-checked that:

✔ you've traced out all the pieces, including any pieces that have to be cut twice

✔ you've used (and marked out) appropriately any pattern pieces marked 'cut one in reverse'

✔ the pile of the mohair is in the right direction – check just one more time

✔ you've marked the opening in seams for stuffing

✔ you've marked the joint positions

✔ you've marked the eye positions, if you're using safety eyes

✔ you're using the suedette, not the mohair, for the paws and pads

These are all very common problems I come across in my workshops; if they're sorted out or avoided at this stage, it makes the assembly of the bear much more likely to be dead easy and stress free.

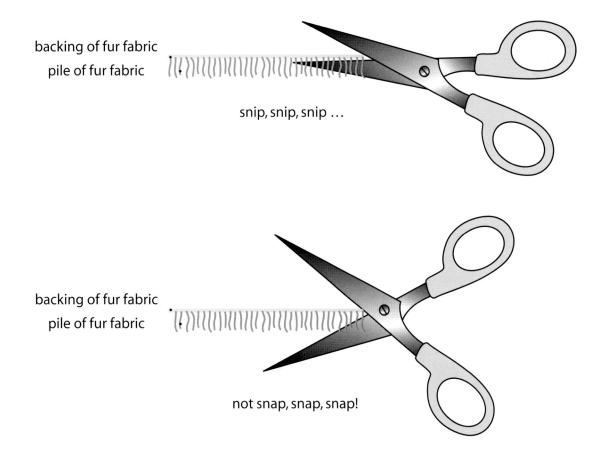

backing of fur fabric
pile of fur fabric

snip, snip, snip …

backing of fur fabric
pile of fur fabric

not snap, snap, snap!

Assembling your Bear

 No fine needlework is needed in teddy bear making; the pile of the mohair covers a multitude of sins. Also, any discrepancies in the seams just add character. I remember one student whose needle skills were dreadful, but who made the best ted I've ever seen: the ears were odd and so were the eyes, the legs were different lengths, and stuffing popped out all over the place, but it beat the socks off a perfect ted for character. It oozed the need for a loving home ...

✪ Sewing by Machine ✪

A few points before you begin:

➤ the secret of joining the pattern pieces together successfully is the pinning. You don't need to tack – just pin well. The mohair, being shiny, will slip and slide all over the place if you don't. Some people panic about sewing over the pins, especially if you are a dressmaker who isn't used to pinning at right angles to the seam, but please be assured that your needle is unlikely to break unless you stitch at 100 miles an hour.

➤ all your stitching needs to be secured at the beginning and at the end of each seam by doing a few reverse stitches on your machine. Hand-tying the ends isn't strong enough.

➤ use a ¼in (5mm) seam for all the patterns (bears and clothes) in this book, unless specified.

➤ wind your bobbin with the same thread you're using for the top, and set your stitch length to 1.5-2. This is smaller than your normal stitch, and provides extra strength in the seams when you're stuffing (it will also make the seams a lot more difficult to unpick, so no mistakes from now on!).

✪ Sewing by Hand ✪

Of course there's no reason why you can't use hand-sewing for assembling your bear. Stitching by hand will make the process slower, and perhaps

your final bear will be a little less strong, but the results will be more or less the same. A small neat backstitch with a quilting thread, which is stronger than ordinary thread, works very well for the seams.

So, let's begin.

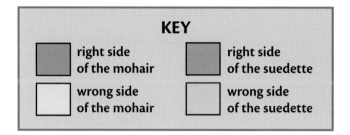

KEY

	right side of the mohair		right side of the suedette
	wrong side of the mohair		wrong side of the suedette

✪ The Body ✪

1 Begin by sewing the darts – one on each side of the body (**a**); place the fabric right sides together and sew across the seam.

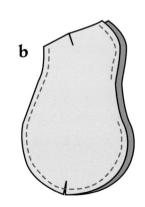

2 Now put the two body parts right sides together and sew all the way round the edges, remembering to leave an opening in the back and the neck (**b**). (These are marked on the pattern, and should now be marked on your fabric pieces.)

❧ HANDY HINT ❧

It's a very common error in workshops not to trust the expert and to sew up the back, thinking that you can stuff via the neck. But - what happens when the head is on though?! Another common error is mixing up the tummy with the back. (How can they? I hear you cry. Everyone knows that the tummy is always rounder.)

✪ The Arms ✪

1 Sew the paw pads to the bottom of the inner arm. Place the pad and arm pieces right sides together (**a**), checking which is the right side of the suedette.

2 Now sew the outer and inner arm together, remembering to pin well (of course), and to leave an opening at the back where marked (**b**). Try to make the sewing nice and smooth around the curve of the paw.

Trim away ⅛in (2.5mm) around the paw; I prefer this to clipping as I have seen so many students clip into the stitch and not realise until they come to stuff the bear. (I don't mean to check up on you at this point, but just double-check that you've have marked the joint placements? Ta.)

Turn the arms right way out (**c**).

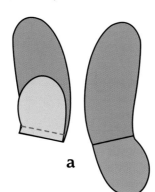

a

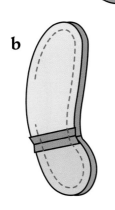

b

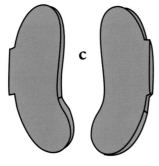

c

✪ The Legs ✪

1 There are two different types of leg in this book.

Charlie's and Rosie's legs are all in one and just need to be folded in half (right sides together), pinned well, and sewn from the top to the toe, remembering to leave a gap in the shin for stuffing (**a**). Don't sew along the bottom (it has been done!) It's advisable to double-sew the inside ankle joint for strength. Trim the ankle curve to ⅛in (2.5mm).

For the other bears you will have two pattern pieces for each leg. To make these up, place the fabric pieces right sides together and pin all the way around the edges, leaving a gap in the **back** of the leg for stuffing (**b**). Don't sew across the bottom of the foot. Double-sew the inside ankle, and trim the ankle curve.

Now let's get these pads out of the way. These will go in beautifully if you follow my instructions carefully.

2 Mark the toe and the heel of the leg with a pin (**c**). Fold your footpad in half lengthways and mark the toe and heel positions with pins (**d**).

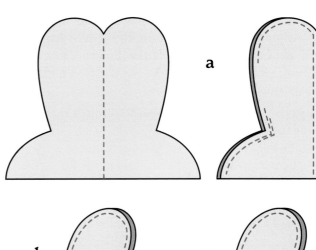

a

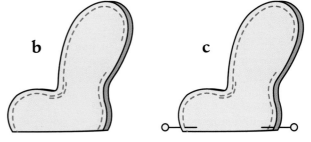

b   **c**

d

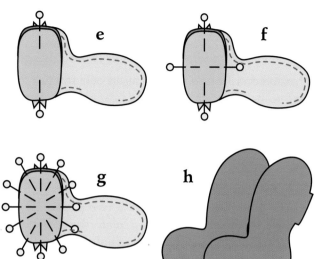

KEY		

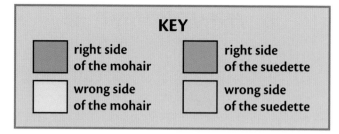

KEY

■ right side of the mohair   ■ right side of the suedette
□ wrong side of the mohair   □ wrong side of the suedette

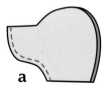

3 With the right sides of the fabric together and your seams open, pin the pad to the toe and then the heel of the leg, matching up the pins (**e**).

Important: the pins should be on the underside of the foot and at right angles to the seam.

4 Now pin east and then west of the foot (**f**). With these anchoring pins in place, you can now fill in all the rest of the pad with pins (**g**).

5 Turn the leg over so that it's standing up, then slowly and carefully sew over all the pins (they should be under the foot at this point). Use a ¼in (5mm) seam, and don't take out the pins until you have finished.

Repeat with the other leg; turn both legs right side out (**h**).

✪ The Head ✪

1 Pin and join the two head pieces together from the nose down to the neck as shown in **a** (if you've lost the position of the nose, check on the template).

2 Familiarise yourself with the head gusset; you'll find a nose and a neck end (**b**). Fold the nose end in half lengthways, and mark the centre with a pin (**c**).

3 Pin this centre mark to the opened centre seam of the head (the one you've just sewn), right sides together (**d**).

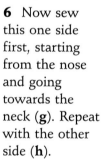

neck

b

nose

4 Pin the neck end of the gusset, one side only, to the neck end of the head (**e**).

5 Now put pins between these two points, gently easing the fabric to fit (**f**). I promise you it does fit, and is much easier when you pin at each end first. I know, because I've been there when I've had to unpick ....

6 Now sew this one side first, starting from the nose and going towards the neck (**g**). Repeat with the other side (**h**).

7 If your seams were an accurate ¼in (5mm) there's no need to trim, but if you were a bit heavy-handed here (and for some reason it's a common area to be so), trim them to ¼in (5mm), no less.

Because we have to stuff the head well, trimming more closely may put pressure on the seams.

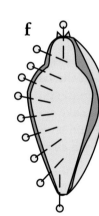
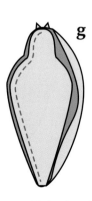

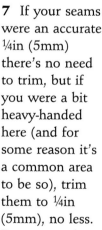

Adding safety eyes

If you're using safety eyes they must be added now. (If you're using buttons as eyes, you'll add these at a slightly later stage, once you've stuffed the head – see below.)

1 Check that the markings for the eyes are exactly opposite each other: if not, adjust. It's quite common for the markings to move when you're sewing the head ... not your fault, of course!

2 Turn the head inside out to check for daylight in the seams (!), or any caught seams. Rectify as necessary.

3 Now you need an awl or **closed** scissors. If you use open scissors, as well as being dangerous, there's every likelihood that you'll tear right across the cheek of the bear. How do I know? Because I've done it – and then the bear needs major repairs before he's even constructed! Use the awl or scissors to make a hole big enough to **force** the eye in place. Don't cut; if you do this is also liable to tear the fabric – just part the weave with force. Place the eye post in the hole and, from the inside, force on the washer.

Stuffing the head

The heads for all the bears need to be stuffed very firmly indeed. This will help maintain their character; we don't want them looking as though they've had a stroke in later years ... Some bears will take nearly a whole bag of stuffing for the head alone.

Tips for stuffing

➤ Most people don't stuff the heads of their bears enough; I always say that the filling has to be 'head hard'.

➤ Push the stuffing in with a wooden dowel or blunt, closed scissors.

➤ Use small amounts at one time – the size of a cotton-wool ball.

➤ The nose and muzzle must be stuffed well, because when you come to embroider the nose you need something good and firm to sew through. You shouldn't be able to pinch the bear's nose.

➤ It's easy to ignore the cheeks, and then the bear starts to resemble a rabbit or rat, so stuff them well also.

Gathering the neck

1 With extra strong thread doubled up and knotted, gather round the neck opening ¼in (5mm) from the edge (**a**). Be sure to secure the start of your sewing line with three stitches sewn on top of each other; you're going to pull very firmly, and you don't want your stitches to snap.

2 Before you pull these stitches up, put part A of the joint into the head with the post poking out (**b**). Gather the stitches up firmly so that no joint is seen at all (**c**). (Sometimes you may have to take a little stuffing out to accommodate the joint.) Fasten off your thread extremely well. These stitches are what will keep your bear's head on for the next hundred years.

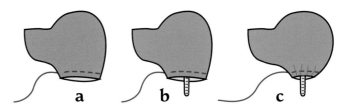

Stitching on the eyes

Now is the best time to sew on your bear's eyes, while you can still manoeuvre the head around well. The positioning of the eyes is very important, and through experience I've come to realise that the ones I least like are those that are too far apart. Even if the eyes are too close they can look good and have lots of character, but far apart is definitely a no-no. I place my bears' eyes just above the bridge of the nose and slightly inside the head seam *(right)*.

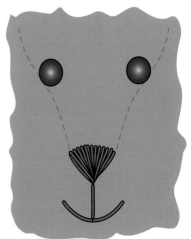

1 It's best to pin the eyes on with glass-headed pins. Sit the bear on a table and go away and look from a distance. Fiddle with the position of the eyes until you're happy. Take the eyes off again and mark the position of each one with a pin.

2 Use your extra-strong thread and a long needle (if you're making Jodie, you need a 5in needle to make it much easier, because her head is bigger;

if you use a smaller needle, it will be almost impossible to get it out at the other side of her head).

3 Cut the thread twice as long as your forearm. Thread the two cut ends into the needle; you'll have a loop at one end. Thread one eye onto the needle and then thread the needle through the loop (**a**); the eye should now be dangling on the thread (**b**).

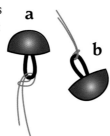

4 With your awl or closed pointed scissors prod a hole into the head at one of the positions you've marked with a pin. The hole has to be big enough to take the loop of the eye. (If the loop is large you can squash it together with a pair of pliers. Be careful not to snap it off, though.)

5 Put the needle into the hole you've just made, and bring it out at the bottom of the neck, being careful to miss the neck joint. Take the needle out and leave the thread dangling (**c**). Repeat this process with the other thread, making sure that you come out of the same hole in the neck; this isn't always as easy as it sounds, and explains why a long needle is essential.

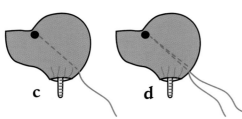

6 When both threads are at the back of the neck (**d**) give them a good tug and you should hear a 'pop' noise when the eye shank goes in the hole. Pulling quite tightly, knot these two threads together several times so that they are thoroughly secure. The knot should pop back into the hole the threads emerge from; if it doesn't, don't worry; the fur should cover up the knot. Look at the eyes and make sure that they're pulled into the head and not loose and dangly.

7 For extra security, so that there is no chance that these eyes will come off, thread one of the strands of cotton back on the needle and sew it back into the hole, coming out somewhere on the side of the head and cut; repeat with the other thread, taking it to the other side of the head. Now repeat the whole process with the other eye.

All this palaver is to ensure the eyes are on securely and are pulled into the head to create a sort of eye socket. Bears with eyes sewn flat on the surface are very dull indeed.

Trimming the muzzle

Once again I consider this an important part of bear making, and it can add great character to your bear's face. The details (*right* and *below*) show the different characters that developed on Jodie's and Rosie's faces through the

way I stitched them. The way you add the features can also make the difference between a boy and a girl bear. Students tend to be nervous about cutting away the fur and go at it like little mice first of all. Be brave and just get stuck in.

➤ The nose area must be trimmed well because when we come to embroider it hair will always poke through, and no-one wants nasal hair problems! So let's start by cutting away the fur from the nose tip, up to the bridge of the nose

where the eyes are. You can trim the fur to ⅛-¼in (2.5-5mm), or once the excess is trimmed off you can use a razor and shave it completely – either option looks very good.

➤ Be sure to pick out any fur in the seams with a needle and trim that away too.

➤ If you want your ted to be a boy, leave him a little goatee beard on the end of the chin – so trim only about an inch down from his nose.

➤ If your ted is to be a girl, trim away unwanted hairs right down to the bottom of the chin and also on the sides of her cheeks.

Embroidering the nose

The nose too is an important area for character-building; a more delicate nose makes for a feminine look, and a large, strong nose is more masculine. In my experience these noses just evolve and you shouldn't worry about them too much. Try not to keep unpicking; it can ruin the shape of the nose and fur – just be happy with what you've been given by the shape of your stitching.

1 These instructions create a basic nose shape. Use two strands of very long thread, at least double the length of your arm, especially for Jodie, and a long needle. Knot the ends of your thread; put the needle in at the neck and come up at the nose.

2 Follow the sequence of diagrams for the nose, making a triangle as a guideline first (**a** and **b**), which you'll gradually fill in (**c**) and finish with a long horizontal stitch (**d**). The most important thing is to keep an even, firm tension. You don't want to pull so tightly that the nose shape distorts, but there again you don't want it so loose that you don't have a smooth nose. (This is where stuffing the nose firmly in the first place helps.)

g

The ears

You may be tempted to worry about exactly where the ears should go, as there are no obvious markings to guide you, but it need not be a problem. Pin the ears in a position towards the front of the head, across a head seam; sit the bear down, and go and make a coffee. Have a good look from afar; if you like what you see, that's where the ears will go, but if something feels or looks wrong, change the ears' positions until you're happy with them.

One of my students made a bear whose ears were very uneven, and I thought it my duty to point this out. She was so delighted with her bear that she felt it was meant to have odd ears, and she didn't want to change them. Her very macho husband thought the bear was so appealing that he refused to let her give it away to their grand-daughter, so she just had to make another one.

a

b

1 Seam the ears, then turn right side out; pin them directly to the head, using a pin at each end of the ear and bending each ear into a slight curve (**a**).

2 Using double thread, sew a securing stitch at one end of one ear. Sew across the back of the ear from right to left using a ladder stitch *(right),* but only catching one side of the ear (**b**). When you come to the end work some securing stitches (remember that teds are often held by their ears).

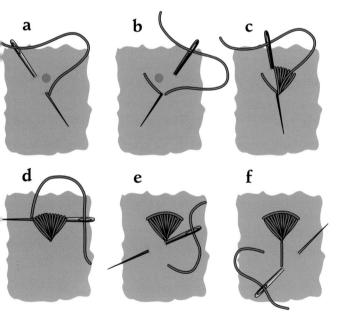

3 Follow the diagrams (**e** and **f**) to stitch the mouth; take a look at the samples in **g** to choose the type of expression you'd like for the mouth. I'm an up-beat type of person and can't make anything that looks sad or angry, but again sometimes these features are out of our control and just happen. That's why no two bears are ever the same.

3 Continue sewing across the front of the ear, using the ladder stitch; this time, only catch the front of the ear. This should create an air pocket in the ear, which prevents a flat, dull look. When you come to the end fasten off securely. Repeat with the other ear.

Voilà! With the most difficult bits finished, we're now on the home run.

✪ *Putting it all together* ✪

Joining the head to the body

1 With the body still inside out, gather round the top of the neck with strong thread ¼in (5mm) from the edge (**a**). Pull the thread up tightly and fasten it off securely. Turn the body out the right way (**b**).

2 Poke the plastic post protruding out of the head through the gathers of the body (**c**). (Even though you've gathered up the neck edge, there will still be room for you to poke the post through.)

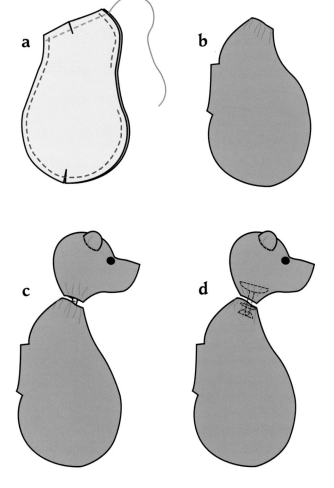

3 Put part B of the joint onto the post in the body (**d**), and then very firmly push on the clip (part C) that holds the joint together. You should hear it click a couple of times.

4 Your bear's head is now in position. You may be wondering why I haven't mentioned sewing it on; the answer is that you don't need to – the joint holds the head in place (**e**).

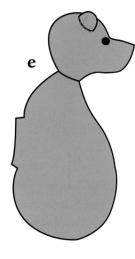

Adding the arms and legs

1 Make a hole in the inner arm where the joint placement is marked, using an awl or **closed** pointed scissors (**a**). You have to be a bit brutal and make a hole big enough to take the post of the joint. Do the same with all four joint markings in the body (**b**).

2 Push joint part A through the hole inside the arm and then into the hole at the top of the body (**c**). (At this point make sure that the ted can slap his thigh; if he can't, it means you don't have the correct arm on. A very common error.)

3 Put on joint part B, and finally clip on joint part C inside the body. Repeat with the other arm (**d**).

4 The legs are put on in the same fashion, but do beware: it's very easy to put the legs on back to front, and there's no little trick like the thigh-slapping to help you. So don't put joint part C on until you're absolutely sure that the bear's toes are facing the right way (**e**). That is the front. (Just in case you are now getting very tired!)

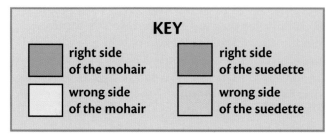

KEY			
▨	right side of the mohair	▨	right side of the suedette
☐	wrong side of the mohair	☐	wrong side of the suedette

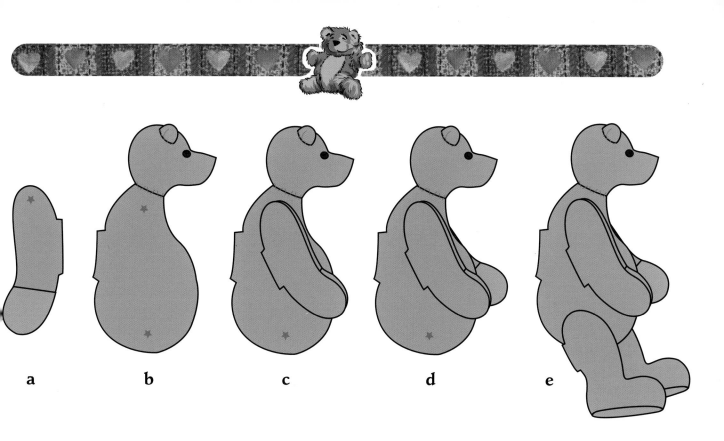

a b c d e

Stuffing

1 Stuff the body first. If you want a nice weighty feel you'll need to put in a bag of plastic pellets. (The amount you'll use will depend on the type of bear you're making; check with each bear's instructions.) Then put conventional stuffing in gently up to the neck. The body does not have to be stuffed as thoroughly as the head.

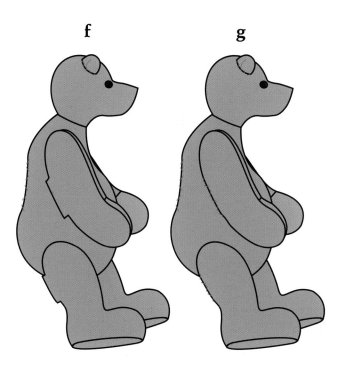

f g

2 If you're going to use a growler you will need to make a space for it; place it in on its side, with the holes facing the back seam, to allow the noise to come out. Don't worry if you think you've been sold the wrong animal; they all sound like cows or sheep, but once they're enclosed within the body they're a little more realistic. (Well, loosely speaking ...!) Close the back seam (**f**) using double thread and a ladder stitch (see page 33).

3 Fill the arms to the wrists with plastic pellets and gently stuff them to the shoulders. Try not to overstuff or they'll look like a body-builder's arms.

4 Fill the legs to the ankles with plastic pellets and then stuff firmly to the thigh.

5 Sew all seams up using the ladder stitch (**g**).

You now need to make friends with your bear – a bit like bonding with a new baby. Find a cosy chair, put on the radio, make a cup of tea, and gently groom your creation all over. Use a needle to pick out any hair that has been caught in the seams, trim any stray hair off the muzzle, and check that the fur around the eyes isn't obstructing the view. Go to your button box and find a nice old pearl button, then sew it discreetly in one ear. Finally, give your bear a gentle brush with a suede brush or even a hairbrush.

Give yourself a pat on the back for making something so lovely. Well done.

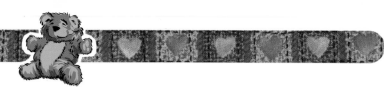

Bear Essentials

The bear is made and looking beautiful, but you've caught that creative bug: the sewing machine is still out, and you want to make something else. Well, this is the chapter for you. I've included patterns for simple clothes for all the bears, designs that you can adapt in lots of different ways and make your very own. You'll also find bed quilts for your teds to snuggle: traditional, dead trendy, and a 'cheater' quilt made using ready-printed fabric. And at the end of the section, a lovely wall-hanging that might stretch your sewing skills just a dash, but will give you and your children so much pleasure, plus – just when you thought you could sew no more – a simple little redwork project. Got that smug smile yet (see page 9)?!

Clothes

 Simple clothes make perfect accessories for treasured bears, so I've designed some garments for several of the bears in this book. I've kept the clothes as easy and quick to make as possible, so if you know any dressmaking rules, forget them now! You don't need clever techniques to create these garments; you can make them look great through your choice of fabrics, and the ways in which you embellish and trim them.

Do try and recycle some of your family's old clothing: it feels good to be frugal and adds a very personal and individual touch. After all, we didn't buy these bears from a chain store, and we're not about to dress them as if they came from one. But of course you can cut labels out of clothing and put them into your bear's clothes, especially if your garments came from an exclusive top London store. I have been known to scour charity shops just for buttons and labels!

We'll start with something nice and easy.

♥ MATERIALS ♥

to make a skirt for **Jodie**,
cut a rectangle 40 x 12in (102 x 30cm)

to make a skirt for **Charlie**,
(well, it might be Charlotte ...)
cut a rectangle 30 x 7in (76 x 18cm)

to make a skirt for **Rosie**,
cut a rectangle 24 x 6in (60 x 15cm)

to make a skirt for **Blanche**,
cut a rectangle 24 x 6in (60 x 15cm)

You'll also need:

elastic

matching cotton thread

contrasting embroidery thread (optional)

Skirts

Blanche's skirt is made from an old denim shirt of my husband's. Instead of cutting a rectangle the size I needed, I tore it, which gave me an even frayed edge; this made a lovely decorative hem which I finished off with a large running stitch in a contrasting colour. Floral or checked shirts, dresses and skirts are also ideal.

♥ INSTRUCTIONS ♥

1 Put the short ends of your rectangle right sides together and stitch a small seam by hand or machine (**a**).

2 At the top of the skirt, turn over ¾in (2cm) to the wrong side and press. Tuck under ¼in (5mm) of the turning and press to make a double hem (**b**). Sew two rows of stitching, one at the top of the casing, very near the edge, and one at the bottom, leaving a ¾in (2cm) gap in the stitching to allow you to thread the elastic. (I think this is the worst job of all.) Use a small safety pin attached to the elastic; thread it through the casing, then stitch the ends together securely to gather the waist (**c**).

3 Hem the bottom of the skirt if you don't have a frayed edge. You can also decorate this edge (**d**) with ricrac, braid, a row of embroidery stitches, a running stitch, or a little row of buttons.

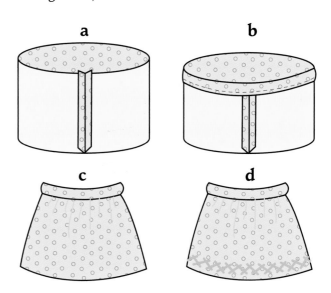

Pockets

If you wish, attach a little pocket cut from a piece of spare material or a contrasting piece (**e**); stitch it on by hand or machine. To make it easier instead of turning under ¼in (5mm) seam allowance all the way around a small square, I always cut a rectangle (**f**). Fold it in half right sides together, and sew around all three raw-edged sides, leaving a gap for turning in the opposite side to the fold (**g**). Trim off your corners and turn the resulting square inside out. Make sure you use the folded edge as the top of the pocket, and either top-stitch or blanket-stitch it in place (**h**).

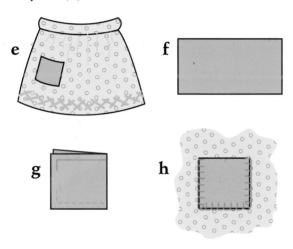

Variations

➤ Make the skirt any length you like, from mini to maxi (that shows my age!)

➤ Decorate the hem.

➤ Make a bib (the same way as you would make a pocket) and two straps to create a pinafore dress; the straps could be ribbon, or ties from a recycled skirt or dress.

Trousers, Shorts, Pyjama Bottoms, Panties

All of these can be created from one pattern; wouldn't it be lovely if it was this easy for us humans?

Cottons or poly/cottons are always the best for quick and easy sewing. Soft denim, the kind they use in skirts or shirts, is fine, but heavy jeans denim is too bulky.

❀ HANDY HINT ❀

*These trousers are lovely and easy to make, but a common error often pops up in my workshops; students sew together the wrong seam. (In fact, I did the costumes for **The King and I** at my local drama group and gave out a pattern very similar to the one here, for the chorus to make their own trousers. Half of them made them correctly; the other half made them with skinny legs and a big bottom.) So, once you've cut out the trousers, do check the pattern to see which seam you should be sewing.*

♥ INSTRUCTIONS ♥

1 Trace or photocopy the relevant pattern piece from the correct bear's collection (see the template pages). Cut out the pattern and use it to cut the trouser pieces as specified (**a** and **b**).

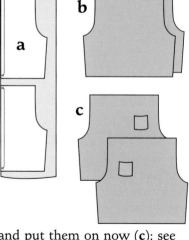

2 If you want pockets on the trousers, decide where they are to go and put them on now (**c**); see above left for tips on making easy pockets.

3 Open out the two trouser pieces and put them right sides together. Sew the two crotch (that word always made me giggle at school) seams (**d**). **This is where you might stitch the wrong seam** (see the tip above); it's the curved one you're doing.

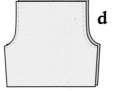

4 Hem both trouser legs while the seam is still open (**e**).

5 Manipulate the trousers so that the two seams you have just sewn are on top of each other; sew the final seam, which is the inside leg (**f**).

6 At the waist, turn over ¾in (2cm) to the inside and tuck under ¼in (5mm) to make a casing for the elastic; stitch the casing and thread the elastic as described for the skirt above (**g**).

Variations

➤ Try making different lengths: shorts, pedal-pushers, midis, bell-bottoms and flares. For panties just make casings around the bottom hems of shorts and thread elastic through.

➤ Add pockets (it's easiest to do this before you assemble the trousers).

➤ Decorate the hems.

➤ Add a bib and straps to create dungarees.

Shirts, Blouses, Pyjama Tops, Cardigans, Jackets, Dressing Gowns

Once again, the same basic pattern can be adapted to create all kinds of different garments. The secret lies in the folding, so be sure you get that bit right.

Soft cotton mixes are ideal fabrics, but fleece is a must for the cardigan and dressing gowns; it's so easy to use, and needs no hemming. You can buy it at most fabric shops and markets – or recycle a fleece a family member has grown out of. (I've just had a thought: wouldn't it be lovely to make a dressing gown out of an old candlewick bedspread? I'm off again ...)

♥ **MATERIALS** ♥

These requirements are for short-length blouses; adjust them as necessary for coats and dressing gowns.

*to make a blouse for **Jodie**, you'll need 20 x 28in (51 x 72cm)*

*to make a shirt for **Charlie**, you'll need 16in (41cm) square*

*to make a blouse for **Rosie**, you'll need 14in (36cm) square; use Blanche's pattern for Rosie's blouse etc*

*to make a blouse for **Blanche**, you'll need 14in (36cm) square*

You'll also need:

buttons

bias binding, lace etc as required for trimming

matching sewing thread

♥ INSTRUCTIONS ♥

1 Fold your fabric in half from top to bottom (**a**); then fold it in half from side to side (**b**). Press.

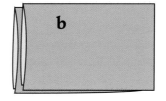

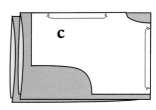

2 Trace or photocopy the relevant pattern piece from the correct bear's collection (see the template pages). Cut out the pattern; lay your pattern piece on top of the folded fabric, making sure you match the folds (**c**). Cut out.

3 While the fabric is still folded, cut the neck opening as indicated on the pattern (**d**).

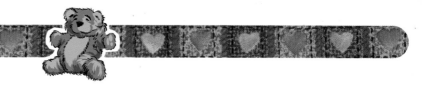

4 Open out the fabric from the first fold only, the side-to-side one (**e**). On **one layer only**, cut up the centre front to the top to create the front opening (**f**).

5 Now all should become clear to you. Sew the two underarm seams and you have a basic top (**g**), which can then be shaped, finished and decorated in a variety of ways.

e

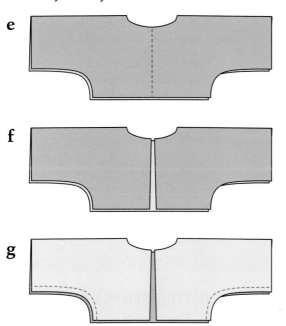

f

g

6 If you're making a bolero-type cardigan or jacket from fleece:

Cut a curved shape on the front two sides only (**h**). Jackets made from fleece don't need hemming, although you can bind the edges if you like. Add pockets if you wish, and fastenings of your choice; try a single button or popper at the top.

7 If you're making a blouse, shirt or pyjama top:

Cut two strips of fabric 1in (2.5cm) wide by the length of the top. With the right sides together, sew a strip down each of the front edges (**i**) to make facings. Don't turn these in the right way at the moment.

h

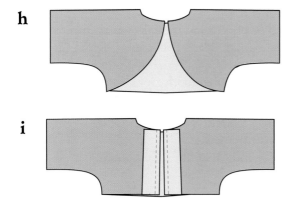

i

Measure the length of the neck opening around the curve and cut a strip slightly longer than this measurement (to allow for the curve) plus seam allowances. Cut the strip twice the width you want the finished collar, again plus seam allowances.

Fold the collar-piece in half lengthways, right sides together, and sew the seam at each end. Turn right way out.

Fold the collar in half to find the centre and pin this to the right side of the centre of the back of the top (**j**). Gently ease the collar round each side (**k**), until you get to the facings. The collar at this point goes under the facing. Sew the collar in place, remembering to sew over the facings at the front. Snip the corners, fold just the seam allowance of the collar to the inside, and turn the facings the right way. Hey presto: a smart little collar and facing (**l**).

j

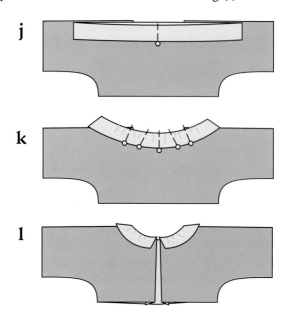

k

l

PHOTO: MARIE STONE

PHOTOS: MARIE STONE

Hem the bottom edge and the sleeves. If you're feeling flash and up for a challenge, make little buttonholes and add buttons – or just sew on poppers or Velcro.

Variations

In my creative mind these seem endless.

➤ Shorten the pattern, without cutting a front opening, and you have a crop top. A little bit longer gives you a peasant blouse; longer still a straight dress, perhaps worn with a belt. Longer still a coat, and even longer a dressing gown. What more can one ted need?

➤ Don't forget those sleeves: a short-sleeved summer blouse or long-sleeved winter one.

➤ Do a basic collar at first, but then start experimenting with frills, lace, pointed ones, contrasting fabrics, or no collar at all.

Dresses

Jodie, Blanche and Rosie all have dresses as part of their wardrobe. For Jodie's and Blanche's dresses we'll use a dressmaking technique where we line the bodice to make the top of the dress, which saves time and makes a nice neat job of the neck and armholes. Use a light- to medium-weight fabric. Rosie's dress is made in a slightly different way –

see page 43. Note that the opening on the dresses is at the front, not the back; on Jodie's the skirt is left without buttons, like an over-dress.

♥ **MATERIALS** ♥

Jodie's & Blanche's Dresses

to make a dress for **Jodie,**
you'll need ¾yd (75cm) of fabric

to make a dress for **Blanche,**
*you'll need a rectangle of roughly 20 x 18in
(50 x 45cm)*

You'll also need:

*matching cotton
three or four buttons and poppers*

♥ **INSTRUCTIONS** ♥

1 Trace or photocopy the dress bodice pattern pieces for the correct bear (see the template pages); paste them onto thin card and cut them out. Use them as templates to cut the fabric pieces (**a**). Cut a rectangle 40 x 12in (102 x 30cm) for the skirt of Jodie's dress, and 20 x 6in (51 x 15cm) for the skirt of Blanche's dress.

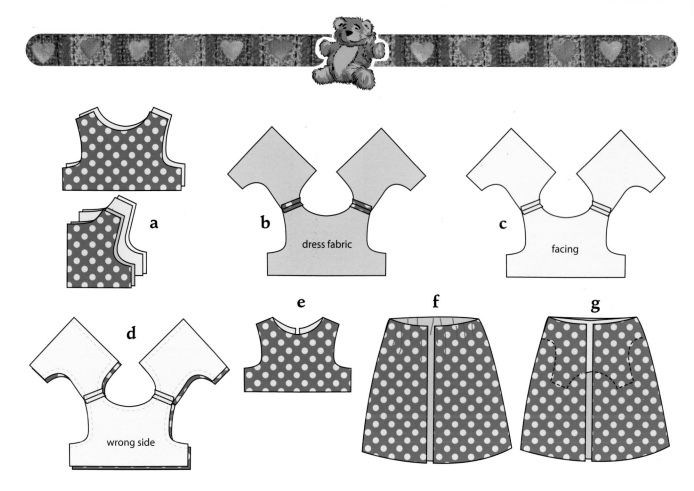

a

b
dress fabric

c
facing

d
wrong side

e

f

g

2 Sew the two front pieces to the back at the shoulder seams; press the seams open (**b**). Repeat with the facing pieces to create a lining (**c**).

3 Lay the dress and the lining on top of each other, right sides together. Match the shoulder seams, and pin the two pieces together.

4 Sew from the bottom of the centre front seam on one side, up and around the neck to the bottom of the other centre front seam. Sew both armholes; don't sew the side seams (**d**).

5 Trim all seams to ⅛in (2-3mm). Now turn the bodice right side out, via one shoulder only (this may be a bit tight on Blanche's dress; just go carefully). Most students don't believe me that it all pulls through one shoulder, and attempts have been made to get each front through each shoulder. It ends up in one big knot: promise.

6 Give the bodice a good press. Open out the top fabric and the lining, and sew the side seams (**e**).

7 Gather the top edge of the skirt (**f**). (I was once taught a wonderful way of gathering. Place a pin at one end of the piece of fabric to be gathered. Using a figure of eight, wrap a length of embroidery thread or crochet cotton around the pin. Zigzag over this piece of cotton along the length of the skirt; pull up the cotton and you have wonderful even gathers.)

8 Pin the wrong side of the gathered skirt to the right side of the lining (**g**). Even out the gathers, and sew in place.

9 Tuck under ¼in (5mm) of the right side of the bodice, and top-stitch the skirt in place.

10 Hem the bottom of the skirt (**h**), then sew on the buttons with poppers underneath them (or make buttonholes if you're feeling keen).

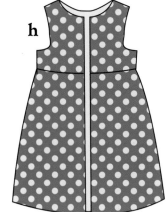

h

Variations

➤ Add a collar to one piece of the bodice before you join them together; make the collar the same way as described for the blouse (see page 40).

➤ Add a piece of lace around the neck, again before you sew the two bodices together.

➤ Add extra pockets.

➤ Just have buttons on the bodice of the dress, so that the skirt front is left open, and make a lace or broderie anglaise petticoat to show in the centre front.

Jodie's dress

PHOTOS: MARIE STONE

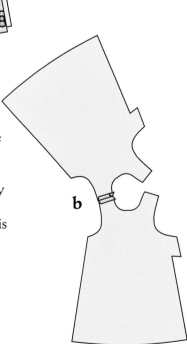

Blanche's dress

Rosie's Shift Dress

A simple dress, created with some hidden dressmaking tricks, so do follow each instruction exactly. (This dress will also fit Blanche.) Use a lightweight cotton fabric, and take ¼in (5mm) seams throughout.

♥ INSTRUCTIONS ♥

1 Trace or photocopy the pattern pieces (see the template pages) and paste them onto thin card. Cut these out and use them as templates to cut the fabric pieces (**a**).

♥ MATERIALS ♥

to make Rosie's dress,
you'll need a fat quarter of cotton fabric

(this dress also fits Blanche, as the two bears are the same height)

You'll also need:
thread
three small buttons and poppers

---

2 Sew the **one** shoulder seam on the dress as indicated on the pattern (**b**); reinforce this seam by sewing twice. (The other shoulder seam is longer, so make sure you get the correct one.) Do the same with the facing shoulder seam; press the seams open.

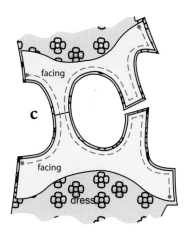

3 Open out the dress and place the facing onto the dress, right sides together, matching the unsewn shoulder seams and neck. Sew around the armholes and the neck (**c**). Trim the seam allowances.

4 Make the pocket by sewing the two pieces all the way around, leaving a gap in the side (**d**). Trim the seams and turn right side out (**e**); press. Fold the pocket in half and sew it ¼in (5mm) down from the top; this forms a little pleat (**f**). Pin the pocket in place and top-stitch it onto the dress.

5 The next bit is slightly tricky, but will save you tons of time by not having to turn under all those fiddly neck seams, so do be patient. Take the bottom corner of the dress and, with blunt-ended scissors, carefully poke it through the hole made by the sewn shoulder seam. Gently pull it through. (This is why I told you to reinforce the seam.) When you've turned it right side out, give it a good press.

6 Sew the side seams, one up to the facing and the other into the facing (**g**). (This sounds odd, but will be much clearer when you actually do it.) Hem the bottom of the dress (**h**).

7 Make a little pleat in the front of the dress and sew on a little button to decorate it.

8 Stitch on buttons and poppers at the shoulder and the side of the dress (**i**).

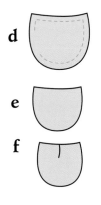
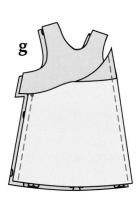

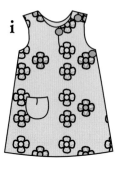

PHOTO: MARIE STONE

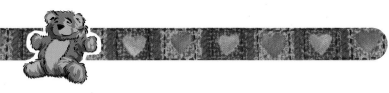

Bedding

No bed – not even a teddy bear's – is complete without a little bit of bedding (above)! At this stage I get ridiculous, and fiddle about for hours making cute things. In this section you'll find three ideas for simple quilts that any bear would appreciate at bedtime.

Blanche's Wholecloth Quilt

For this quilt (see overleaf) I used a piece of blue silk; it reminded me of the counterpanes my grandmother had on her bed. Silk is wonderful to quilt, and it only took me the length of a Sunday afternoon film to sew. Lighter-coloured fabrics are easier to trace through; an old cotton shirt or dress, or an old silk shirt, would be ideal. Have a hunt and you'll probably find something to recycle.

♥ MATERIALS ♥

two pieces of lightweight fabric 12 x 10in (30 x 25cm), plus extra strips for binding

one piece of wadding 12 x 10in (30 x 25cm)

reel of cotton the same colour as your fabric quilting cotton is ideal, but ordinary will be OK for this small project

pencil or fade-away pen
(be sure to check, by testing on a scrap piece of fabric, especially if you're using silk; fade-away pens really do fade)

PHOTO: LYNSEY PIFF

♥ INSTRUCTIONS ♥

1 Trace or photocopy the pattern from page 94, and trace the design onto your fabric. (You may find it easier to trace by sticking the photocopy to a window and then sticking the fabric on top; the light will help you to see through the fabric better.)

2 Tape all four corners of your backing fabric onto a table so that it's nice and taut. Place your wadding on top, smoothing it out nicely; finally put the marked fabric on top, marked side up. Use safety pins to pin the quilt together every two to three inches, going through to the backing fabric. (If you don't have any safety pins to hand, you can tack every two inches.)

3 You're now ready to sew the quilt with a small, even running stitch. Begin with a small knot in the end of your thread; when you give a little tug it will hide neatly between the two layers of the quilt. End each line of sewing with a backstitch and weave the thread between the two layers, coming out about an inch away from the last stitch; this way you won't have any knots on the back.

4 To bind the edges of the quilt cut strips of fabric 1¼in (3cm) wide. Press under ¼in (5mm) at one end and then iron the strip in half lengthways, wrong sides together. Place the binding half way

down the right side of the quilt, right sides together and matching the raw edges, and attach the binding to the quilt, then fold it to the back and slipstitch it in place. (If you're not sure how to do this, the process is shown in detail on the *Goodnight, Sleep Tight!* wall-hanging on page 51; follow steps 10-12.)

Charlie's Quilt

This is a nice and easy rough and tumbly quilt for a very scruffy bear. It's made from denims; check out the charity shops or have a good clear-out. I used about four different types of denim, and used the wrong sides too for yet more colours. You need a lightweight contrasting fabric to go in the middle of the quilt; this only shows at the seam edge, so don't use anything special. I used one of my daughter's old check dresses. You also need a third contrast fabric, for the small squares and binding strips; I used an old shirt of my husband's (yes, he does have some left).

Buttons are another passion of mine, and I've used some on this quilt; I used old linen ones, but pearl or old shirt buttons are fine. Lots of the instructions on this quilt go against the grain; trust me, it will turn out fine once it's been through the washing process.

♥ MATERIALS ♥

twenty-four 6in (15cm) squares of assorted lightweight denims (it's important to cut them accurately)

twelve 6in (15cm) squares of contrasting fabric

12 x 24in (30 x 60cm) rectangle of fabric, from which you will cut out twelve 2in (5cm) squares, and cut or tear four 1 x 24in (2.5 x 60cm) strips

twelve buttons

jeans needle, size 16, for your machine

♥ INSTRUCTIONS ♥

1 Lay out twelve of the denim squares on the table and move them around until you're happy with the colour arrangement. Do the same with the squares that are to go on the back.

5 Place one of your little 2in (5cm) squares in the middle of each block; with knots showing and chunky stitches, sew them in place through all three layers, sewing the buttons on last (**d**).

6 It's looking a mess, and you're worried; don't worry – all will be fine. Take a pair of sharp scissors and snip into all the seams every half inch, including the edging. Pop the quilt into the washing machine, on an economy wash; then throw it in the tumble dryer and hey presto! Charlie has one of the most trendy quilts around.

One last little tip: empty the filter of the tumble dryer.

Jodie's Quilt

When you took a look at the photograph of Jodie's quilt, I bet you thought 'I'm not sewing all those little squares together!' Now, would I do that to you? It's about time we cheated and made something really quickly. The fabric in the centre of the quilt – the one with all the little squares – is in fact a whole piece of cloth with the design printed on it. If you can visit a quilt shop they nearly always stock some fabric that already looks like a pieced quilt top. If you live too far away, phone and describe what you need and most of them will send it the next day. It's lovely getting something in the post. If you really can't wait, any checked fabric whose squares are symmetrical is ideal.

Instead of layering the quilt with three layers, as we do traditionally, we'll just use fleece for the backing.

♥ MATERIALS ♥

roughly 18 x 10in (45 x 25cm) pre-printed patchwork fabric

roughly 7 x 45in (18 x 114cm) plain contrasting fabric for the borders

2½in (6cm) wide strip of fabric for binding, roughly 80in (2m) long

roughly 21 x 15in (54 x 38cm) fleece

matching thread

2 Make little 'jam sandwiches' (the jam being the lining, and the bread on each side being the denim) with the squares, being careful to keep them in the right order front and back. Pin the three layers of each square together on all four sides (**a**).

3 Join the little sandwiches to each other, in rows of three, with the **backs** of the squares facing each other (**b**). Sew slowly, because you're sewing through six layers. When you've sewn four rows of three, start joining the rows together, trying to match the seams, again with wrong sides together. Feels odd, doesn't it?

4 Sew long strips of fabric along the top and bottom edges, stitching through the middle of the strip (**c**). Trim to size. Finger-press the strip in half, away from the quilt, and repeat with the other two sides.

PHOTO: LYNSEY PIFF

Fleece is now readily available in most fabric shops and markets – or use an old fleecy jumper.

Try this technique for your bear's bed quilt, but keep in mind too that a larger size makes a great pram rug, throw for the sofa or even a bed quilt. The use of fleece is a bit frowned on by traditional quilters, but do we mind? Snugability is the essence of this type of quilt.

Some traditional quilts I've made may provide warmth but aren't always cosy to the touch; ones like this with fleece on the back are just lovely. They machine-quilt well, as long as the needle is sharp, and hold their shape. If you like, take this little quilt a step further and experiment with different designs of fabric and different kinds of embellishment; as I'm always saying, 'from little acorns, mighty oaks do grow'.

♥ INSTRUCTIONS ♥

1 To achieve a professional look (so that no-one can see we cheated!), you need to cut your fabric ¼in (5mm) beyond the line of squares round the edges. This will give you a seam allowance, so that all the squares will look like true patchwork squares when the quilt is sewn. (This also means that all measurements I give you are approximate, as the final measurements will depend on the type of squares in your quilt.) If you're using a regular checked fabric such as gingham, allow four squares of large-weave gingham for each patch, and one square around all four sides for the seam allowance.

2 From the border strip, cut two lengths to fit the two long sides of your quilt and sew them in place over your seam allowance. Press the seams open.

3 Cut two more strips for the top and bottom of the quilt, and attach them in the same way.

4 Tape the four corners of the fleece onto a table top, and place the quilt on top, right side up; smooth out any wrinkles, and safety-pin the two layers together, pinning every three inches or slightly closer.

5 Now quilt along the lines of the squares. Hand quilting is just a running stitch, or you can quilt by machine, which is obviously faster. Don't sew each square individually; go up and down the quilt in lines.

❀ *HANDY HINT* ❀

If you want to quilt by hand and own any specialised hand-quilting thread, use this; if not, run ordinary thread through a candle to coat it with a little wax and this will prevent the thread from knotting while sewing. If you're using a machine, then ordinary thread is fine, but remember that you'll need a nice new sharp needle.

6 If there are any extra designs on the fabric, you could quilt or appliqué these too; I stitched a few of the heart motifs from my fabric along the border to create a nice finish.

7 Bind the quilt using the method described for *Goodnight, Sleep Tight!* (see page 51).

8 It's really important to label your quilt with your name, the date and who it was made for, so that the historians who find it in a hundred years' time will have all the details!

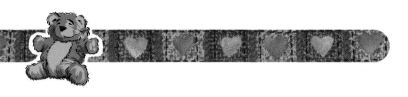

Goodnight, Sleep Tight!

This is a simple little wall-hanging that has given my children enormous pleasure in turn at bed-times; I hang it on the wall near the child's pillow so that he or she can play with it. I even adapted the design and made it into a little house, and then went one step further and made a large Christmas advent calendar with twenty-four little beds. (Do I ever sleep myself, I hear you cry! The answer is: soundly.)

Once again, this wall-hanging can be made out of lots of scraps. Recycle your children's clothes; I used a gingham school uniform. You'll be surprised at the wonderful memories your children or grandchildren will have when, in years to come, they find these things you've made in the bottom of an old drawer.

With this design, it's very important to cut and sew accurately. If you have a rotary cutter, mat and ruler use these. If you have a ¼in foot on your sewing machine this will help to keep your seams accurate. Take care and a bit of time, and the wall-hanging will fit together well. Spray-starch all your fabric, because this will make the folding nice and sharp.

I've included some simple quilting on this hanging; this can be done by hand or machine. Hand quilting is just a small running stitch to hold all three layers together; if you're quilting by machine, simply use an ordinary straight stitch.

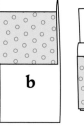

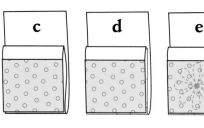

♥ MATERIALS ♥

three 4½ x 11½in (11.5 x 29cm) rectangles of white cotton sheeting

three 4½ x 3½in (11.5 x 9cm) rectangles of patterned cotton fabric for the quilts

three 4½ in (11.5cm) squares of wadding

lightweight denim for the inside borders:

four 1½ x 6½in (4 x 17cm) strips

one 2½ x 16½in (6.5 x 42cm) strip

one 3½ x 16½in (9 x 42cm) strip

contrasting fabric for the outside borders:

two 11½ x 1½in (29 x 4cm) strips

two 19½ x 1½in (50 x 4cm) strips

roughly 22 x 17in (56 x 43cm) wadding

roughly 23 x 18in (59 x 46cm) backing fabric

2yd (2m) of binding, 2in (5cm) wide
(make this from strips cut across the width of the fabric from selvedge to selvedge; the strips can be joined)

reel of matching cotton

skein of embroidery thread

spray starch

20 safety pins

♥ INSTRUCTIONS ♥

1 Position one of the quilt top fabrics at the top of one piece of sheeting, right sides together. Stitch the seam between them, and press the seam towards the quilt fabric. You now have a rectangle of white fabric with a patterned piece at one end (**a**). Repeat this process with the other two quilt fabrics and pieces of sheeting.

2 On each quilt, make a fold in the sheeting 1in (2.5cm) away from the quilt fabric (**b**). Now fold the sheeting level with the bottom of the quilt fabric, back up to the top (**c**). This creates a complete 'bed' consisting of a quilt, a top sheet and a bottom sheet; tack down the two sides to keep the pieces in place. Repeat with the two other beds.

3 Place the square of wadding between the top sheet and the bed cover (**d**). You can now quilt the bed cover if you wish, by hand or machine (**e**).

4 Sew the row of beds together using the 1½ x 6½in (4 x 17cm) strips (**f**), and add a strip at each side. You have quite a few layers to go through so be careful and sew slowly. (If you have a walking foot attachment for your machine, use it for this stage.) Press the seams to one side.

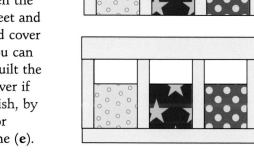

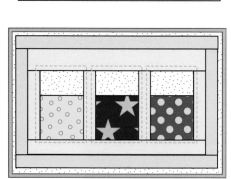

5 Attach the remaining narrow strip to the bottom of the quilt and the wider one to the top (**g**). Press.

6 Now attach the outside border: sew the two side strips on first, and then the top and bottom ones (**h**). Press.

7 Tape the backing fabric to a table, smooth out the wadding on top, and place your work on top of this, right side up. Pin all three layers together with safety pins, and quilt by hand or machine around all three beds (**i**).

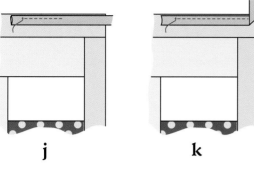

j   **k**   **l**

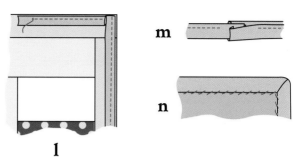

m

n

8 Using ordinary pins, pin the edges of the quilt together so that they can't move. Using a large stitch, sew around the edge less than ¼in (5mm) from the edge. Now you can cut away all the excess wadding and backing; make sure that the quilt is square by using your rotary board, cutter and ruler if you have one.

9 Fold the binding in half along its length and press. Lay it along one edge of the quilt, matching the raw edges.

10 Start on one side of your quilt, ½in (1cm) from the end of the binding, and sew the binding on using a ¼in (5mm) seam (**j**). Stitch until you come to an exact ¼in (5mm) from the end of one corner (you may want to mark the position with a pin). Pull the work away from the machine and fold the binding up and away from you, so that it's aligned with the edge of the quilt (**k**). Holding the corner, fold the binding back down, aligning it with the raw edge of the quilt (**l**); pin in position. Sew straight down this side until you reach the next corner, and repeat the process.

11 When you've reached your starting point, turn under ¼in (5mm) at the start of the binding, tuck the other end of the binding strip into the fold (**m**), trim to size and then sew right over the top.

12 The binding will now fold over to the back of the hanging where you can slipstitch it in place (**n**); the corners will miraculously mitre for you on their own. Finish off the hanging with display loops along the top, or add a hanging sleeve on the back.

You now have the basis of the bed design, and the sky's the limit (or, more likely, time) as to how you decorate your wall-hanging. Rummage through your button tin to find decorative buttons; make little pillows, add lace or braid to the quilt, embroider some words of a favourite bedtime lullaby. Most importantly, make the little teds to go in the beds; they are the Tweeny Beanie Bears (see page 14).

Once you're confident with the initial concept you can go to town and use all your wonderful machine- or hand-sewing skills, and make a more detailed version. You could also enlarge the size of the basic pattern to suit a bigger ted. Increase the numbers of beds (*below*) – or make only one, with a bag handle so that it's portable. Make the beds with an appliquéd headboard, and decorate the walls with pictures. There's no limit to the creative possibilities!

PHOTO: LYNSEY PIFF

Theodore Redwork Hanging

This is a lovely quick little project for those of you who like embroidery. It tucks into a handbag nicely, for times when you're waiting in the school car park or the doctor's surgery; it's also nice and easy for children to do. You may want to have the calico and wadding larger to start with and then cut them to size when you've finished the stitching. Calico works well for this design, or if you can get hold of it from craft shops you could try Onsberg, a nice evenweave fabric produced specially for embroidery.

♥ INSTRUCTIONS ♥

1 Photocopy or trace the pattern on page 95 onto plain paper.

2 With a sharp pencil, trace the pattern onto your calico. (You may find it easier to tape the photocopy to the window on a sunny day, and then tape the calico on top; you'll then be able to see better to trace).

♥ MATERIALS ♥

11½ x 9½in (29 x 24cm) calico or Onsberg

11½ x 9½in (29 x 24cm) wadding (I always prefer cotton wadding)

12½ x 10½in (32 x 27cm) backing fabric (which will show on the front, too)

skein of red coton à broder or embroidery thread

spray starch

3 Pin the marked calico to the piece of wadding, right side up. Using the red thread, quilt round the design on the traced line, using a running stitch or a backstitch. Stitch through both layers, and keep all knots at the back of the work.

4 When all the quilting is complete, cut the calico to the correct size if you haven't already done so.

5 Spray the backing fabric thoroughly with spray starch so that you will get a good crease, and iron flat.

6 Lay the backing fabric right side down on a flat surface. Position the design in the centre, right side up, making sure you have an equal allowance of backing fabric on all four sides.

7 Starting with one corner of the backing fabric, fold the point in to meet the point of the calico corner (**a**). Fold this onto the calico and finger-press, then pin (**b**). Repeat with the other three corners.

8 Fold the top, bottom and sides over, tucking under ¼in (5mm) of the raw edge (**c**). Finger-press the edges and pin in place (you may even want to tack).

9 You can now either slipstitch the sides in place (**d**) or topstitch them by machine with a contrasting thread, depending on how neat you are. (You don't often hear me use that word, neat.)

There you are; all finished and done.

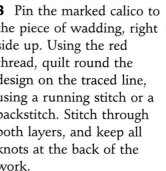

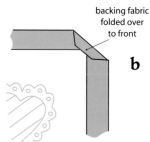

corner of backing fabric folded over

backing fabric

quilt

a

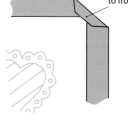

backing fabric folded over to front

b

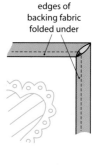

edges of backing fabric folded under

c

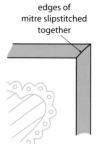

edges of mitre slipstitched together

d

The Shoebox Bear

Once there was a little girl called Harriet. Harriet was eight years old and lived with her mum and dad in a nice house in the country. Harriet's dad was in the army and sometimes had to do overseas duty; Harriet was feeling sad because her Dad had to go away again – this time for several months.

The night before he went he brought home a present: it was a teddy bear. 'This is to keep you company until I come home again,' he said. Harriet gave the bear a big cuddle, which made her feel much more cheerful.

Meanwhile, Harriet's Nanny had made a teddy in one of Mandy's workshops; she didn't know about the other teddy, and gave her one to Harriet, thinking it would help her not to miss her dad too much. Harriet decided to call the first one Jodie and the second one Charlie, and she loved them both very much.

Her dad wrote her letters about the country where he had been sent, and the sad life some of the children had in refugee camps, with no toys and not really enough food. He said there was one girl who reminded him of Harriet.

At school Harriet's class was working on a project about the problems of children around the world, so Harriet suggested that perhaps they could do something for the children where her dad's unit was based.

Her teacher, Mrs Pentin, thought this was a good idea and suggested that each child got a shoebox and put one of their best toys in it; they could then bring it to the class, and she would find a way of getting it to the children.

Harriet ran home from school very excited about this idea and told her mum, who in turn told her dad when he phoned that night. He said there would be no problem about getting the boxes to the children, as his unit would do it.

The next day Harriet and her mum went to the shoe shop and got a nice solid box.

Harriet decided to ask Nanny if she could send Charlie to a little child across the sea. Nanny thought it was a lovely idea – and very kind of Harriet.

Harriet and her mum got to work and made the inside of the box like a little bed with a pillow and blankets; Nanny made some pyjamas for Charlie's travelling gear. Harriet felt quite sad to say 'goodbye' when she put the lid on the box, but cheered up when Nanny said she could make her another bear at Mandy's next workshop. She told Harriet how happy the little girl who received the box would be when she opened it and found Charlie.

There was great excitement at the school when a big army truck arrived to collect the boxes. A few weeks later there was even more excitement when a letter and some pictures arrived; these had been drawn by the children who had been so happy to receive the shoebox presents.

Harriet's dad had become fond of the little girl in the refugee camp who reminded him of Harriet. Her name was Phoebe, and when he found out that both her parents had been killed and she was an orphan, he talked to Harriet's mum about adopting Phoebe as a sister for Harriet. When all the legal paperwork was done, Harriet's mum was able to tell Harriet about her new playmate who would be coming to join the family.

When the day finally arrived and Phoebe came to live at Harriet's house, Phoebe was very shy at first – that is, until Harriet introduced her to Jodie! Then a big smile lit up Phoebe's face. She went to her bag, opened it up and – guess what? Inside was a shoebox, and when Phoebe took off the lid, lying there snugly tucked up in his bed was a teddy bear dressed in pyjamas. Yes; it was teddy Charlie. And that's where we'll leave our story, with them all playing happily ever after.

GALLERY

Name

Date of birth

Stitched by

Stitched for

Distinguishing marks

Name

Date of birth

Stitched by

Stitched for

Distinguishing marks

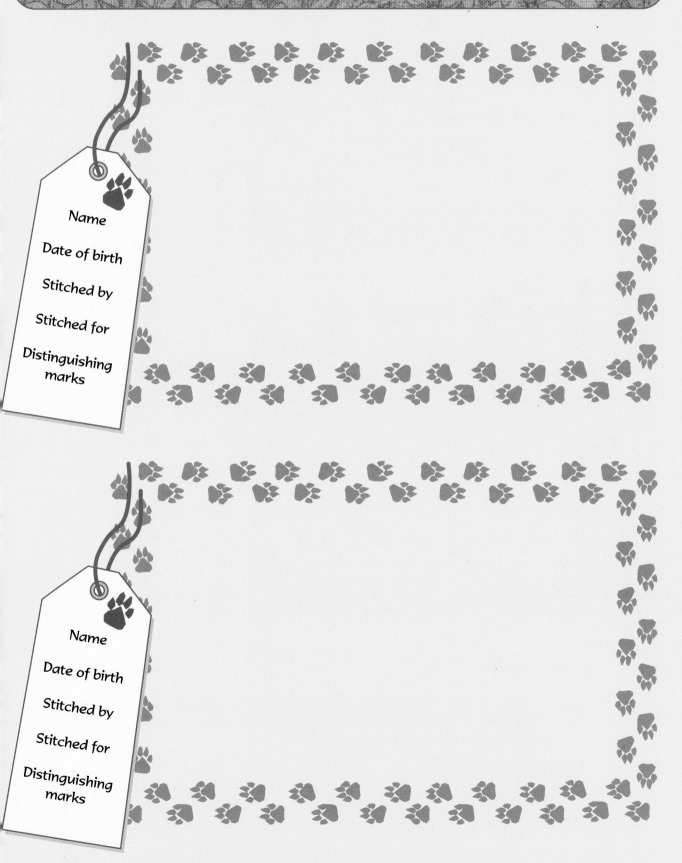

Name

Date of birth

Stitched by

Stitched for

Distinguishing marks

Name

Date of birth

Stitched by

Stitched for

Distinguishing marks

✪ *Supplies & Information* ✪

As you may have guessed by now, I like recycling my family's clothes and scouring charity shops, but I'm also passionate about buying new fabrics. The shops listed below are some of my favourites, and I've included ones that supply specialist bits and pieces for bear-making.

♥ Specialist bear-making supplies ♥

Admiral Bear Supplies
37 Warren Drive, Ruislip, Middlesex HA4 9RD (tel 020 8868 9598; website www.admiral-bears.com)

Oakley Fabrics
8 May Street, Luton, Beds LU1 3QY (tel 01582 424828)
Supplies all your needs for traditional bear-making, from joints, eyes, and mohair fur to stuffing; they have a shop, and also do mail order.

K Craft
Kim Holt, 238 Glynswood, Chard, Somerset TA20 1BG
(tel 01460 66341)
Stocks kunin felt and kunin plush, along with a wonderful array of craft goodies; mail order only.

♥ Fabric for bears' clothes & quilts ♥

Piecemakers
13 Manor Green Road, Epsom, Surrey KT19 8RA (tel 01372 743161; website www.piecemakers.co.uk)
One of my favourite patchwork fabric shops; specialises in the more country and folk fabrics. No mail order, but very helpful staff.

House of Patchwork
Unit 30 Tower Centre, Hoddesdon Herts EN11 8UB (tel 01992 447544; website www.houseofpatchwork.co.uk)
A beautiful collection of patchwork fabrics and accessories, and many interesting workshops, including my own Bear Necessities classes

The Quilt Room
20 West Street, Dorking, Surrey RH41BL (tel 01306 877307; website wwwquiltroom.co.uk)
A large selection of patchwork fabrics, a great catalogue, and mail order service.

Puddleducks
116 St Johns, Sevenoaks, Kent TN13 3PD (tel 01732 743642)
A lovely little shop selling delicious fabrics; they even serve you coffee while you shop!

♥ Places of interest ♥

Grizzly Business: collectable teddybears
Candy Cottage, High Street, Alfriston, East Sussex BN26 5JA
This shop has a wide selection of limited editions and collectors' bears from leading names and artists. A lovely place to browse to get ideas ; the village is also a beautiful place to visit.

Hartfield
In the heart of the Ashdown Forest, Hartfield is where AA Milne (who wrote *Winnie the Pooh*) grew up. In the high street is Pooh Corner, a shop selling everything to do with Pooh. You can pick up a free map in the shop which will direct you to all the enchanted places Milne writes about in his books. A great place to take the family on a Sunday afternoon for a walk, and to play pooh-sticks on the bridge. Visit the website for more details:
www.poohcorner.net

♥ Last, but not least ♥

The Book of the Teddy Bear by Margaret Hutchings, published by Mills and Boon
A treasure of a book, which I'm afraid is now out of print, but keep an eye out for it in second-hand book shops – I've found quite a few copies that way. It's full of lovely diagrams, patterns and stories, all a bit old fashioned, but I love a nostalgic twist. Imagine how excited you'll be if you find one!

♥ Thankyous ♥

➤ My gorgeous and long-suffering husband, *who rarely moans about the teds, dolls, quilts and sewing things that are in every room of our house and have been for the past 22 years!*

➤ My three delightful girls and little boy, *who have given me so much pleasure, for enjoying their home-made gifts and teds, and for helping me out on the computer when I sometimes can't even turn it on …*

➤ My lovely ladies at Needlethreaders, and all my adult education classes, *for their support, encouragement, and for putting up with me with my wild and unusual ideas.*

➤ Jill Pentin, *an effervescent and most productive student, who wrote the story for us all to read to our children and grandchildren.*

➤ Gail and Christopher Lawther, *for their encouraging e-mails, for turning my eccentric scribbles into this wonderful book, and for giving me the opportunity of writing it – another dream fulfilled.*

➤ Marie Stone, *for some of the wonderful photos of the bears. She also deserves a public thankyou for encapsulating my children's childhood in the most precious black and white photos (see right). If you'd like to enquire about Marie's photography, her telephone number is 01323 440544*

➤ Lynsey Piff, *for spending a lovely sunny Sussex day in my garden with me, taking more great photos of the bears. Thankyou.*

♥ And finally … ♥

I dedicate this book to my mum, Joanie, who taught me all my sewing and toy-making skills.

Thankyou Mum.

THE TEMPLATES

PHOTO: MARIE STONE

SIMPLE SIMON
TEMPLATE
mark on
doubled fabric

leave open

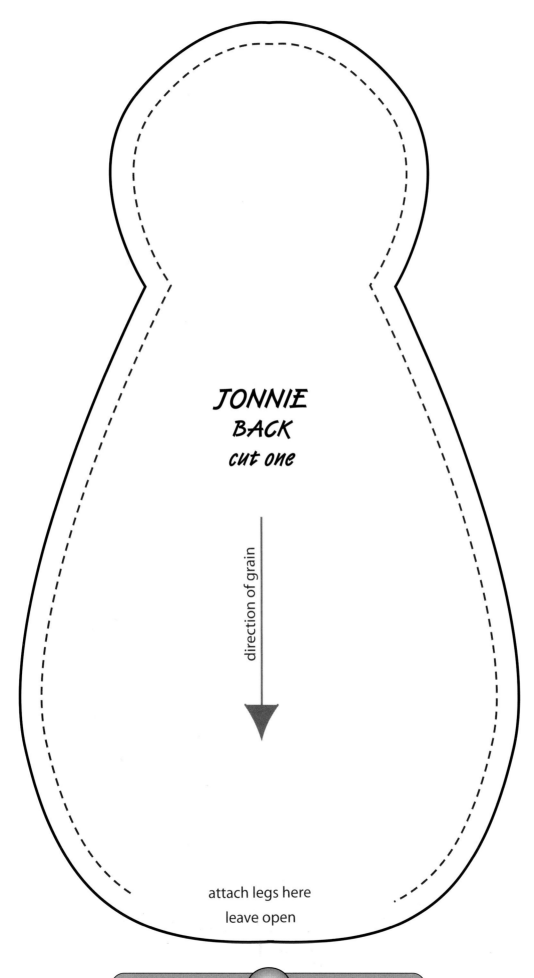

JONNIE
BACK
cut one

direction of grain

attach legs here

leave open

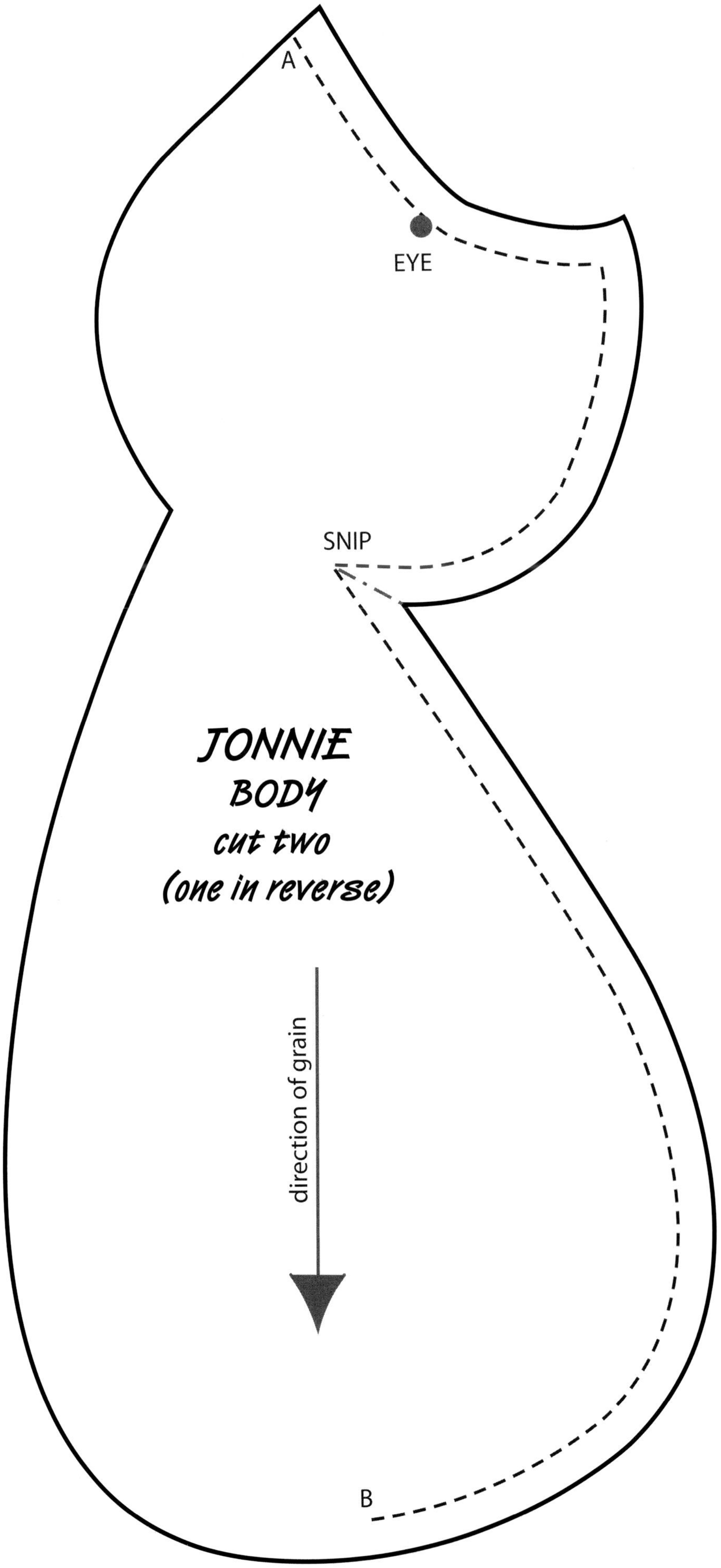

A

EYE

SNIP

JONNIE
BODY
cut two
(one in reverse)

direction of grain

B

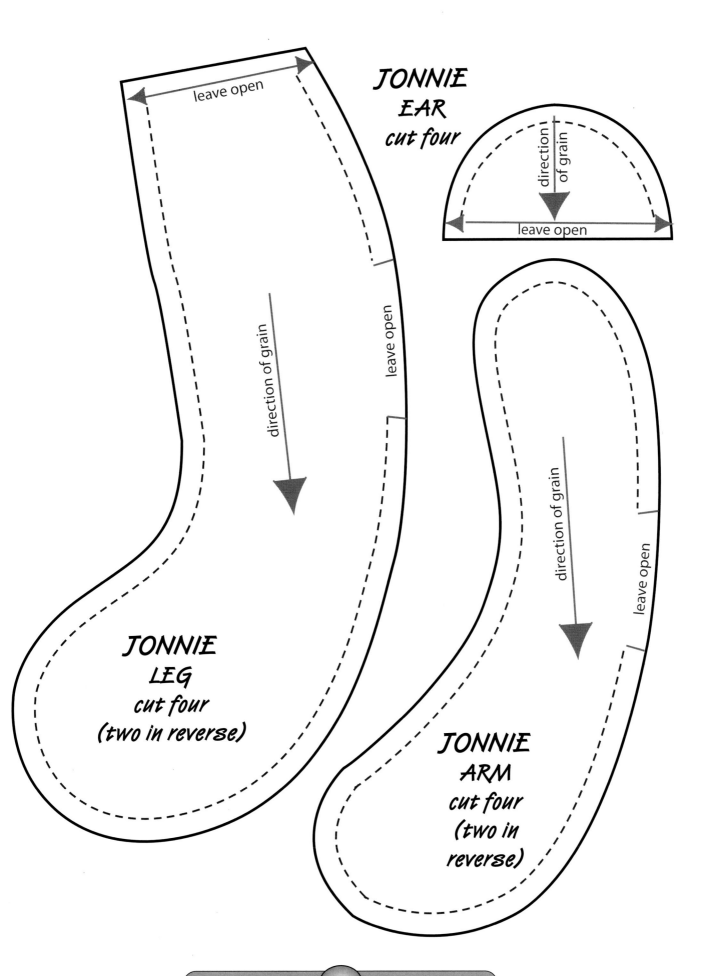

JONNIE
EAR
cut four

leave open

direction
of grain

leave open

direction of grain

leave open

direction of grain

leave open

JONNIE
LEG
cut four
(two in reverse)

JONNIE
ARM
cut four
(two in
reverse)

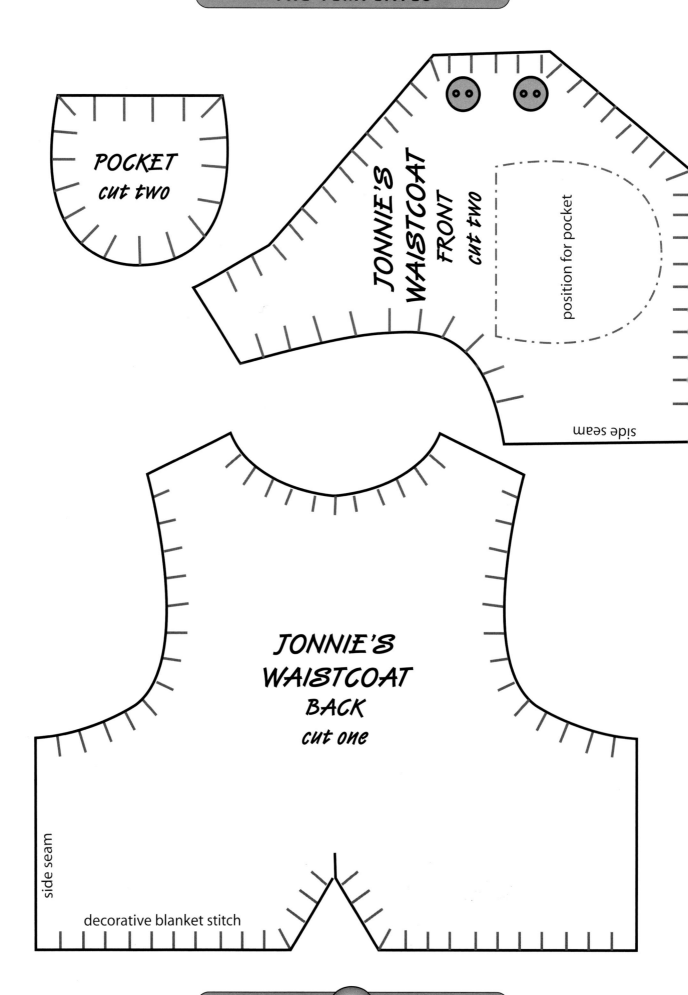

POCKET
cut two

JONNIE'S
WAISTCOAT
FRONT
cut two

position for pocket

side seam

JONNIE'S
WAISTCOAT
BACK
cut one

side seam

decorative blanket stitch

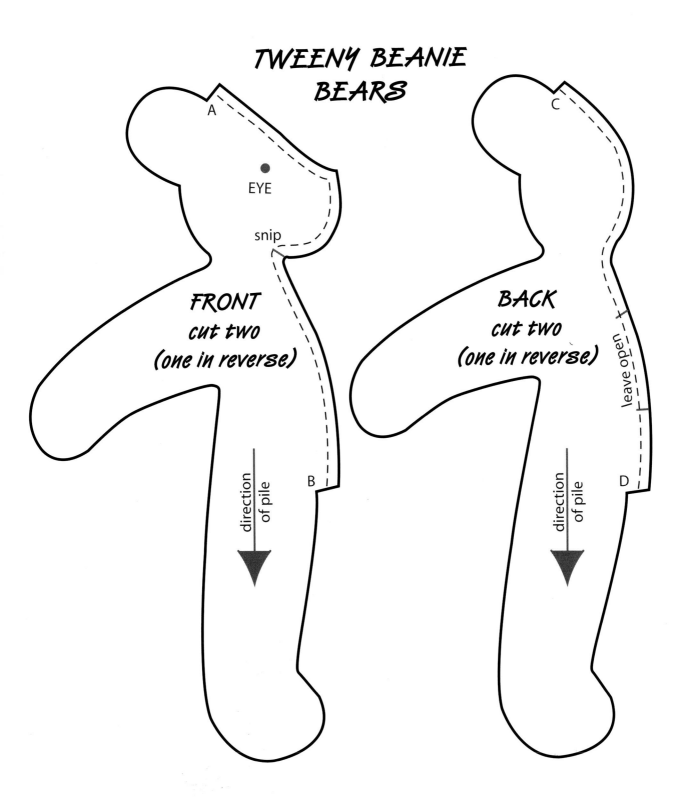

TWEENY BEANIE BEARS

A

EYE

snip

FRONT
cut two
(one in reverse)

direction of pile

B

C

BACK
cut two
(one in reverse)

leave open

direction of pile

D

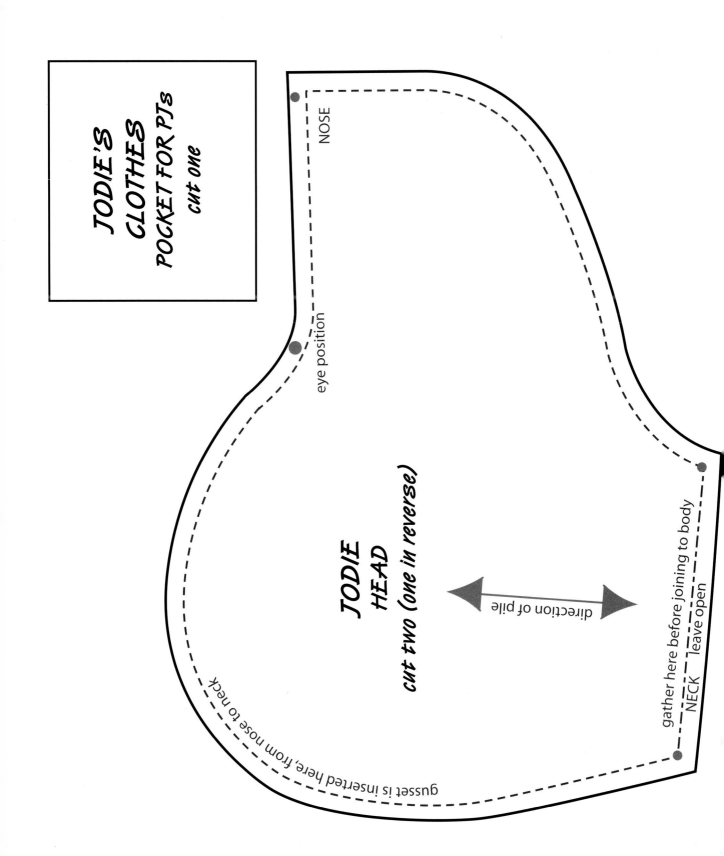

JODIE'S CLOTHES
POCKET FOR PJs
cut one

NOSE

eye position

JODIE
HEAD
cut two (one in reverse)

direction of pile

gusset is inserted here, from nose to neck

gather here before joining to body

NECK leave open

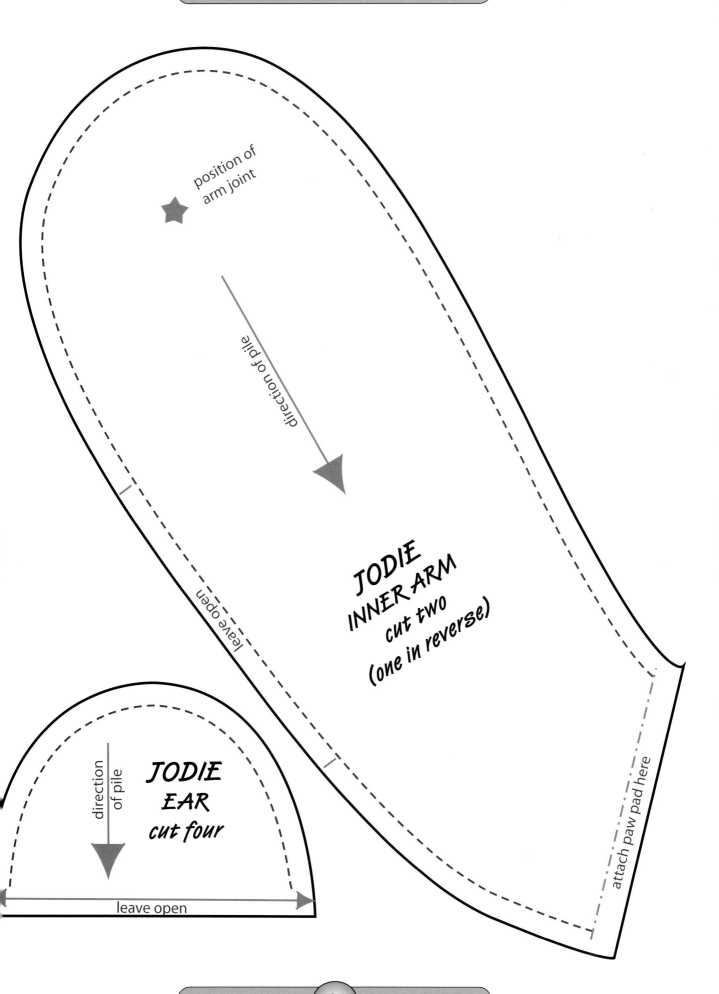

position of
arm joint

direction of pile

JODIE
INNER ARM
cut two
(one in reverse)

leave open

attach paw pad here

direction
of pile

JODIE
EAR
cut four

leave open

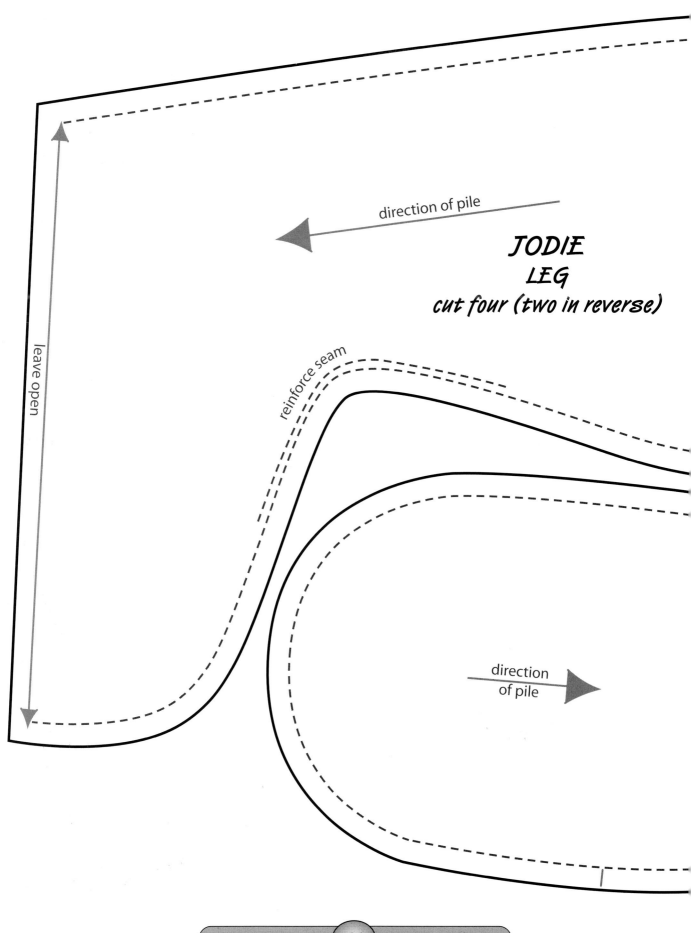

direction of pile

JODIE
LEG
cut four (two in reverse)

leave open

reinforce seam

direction
of pile

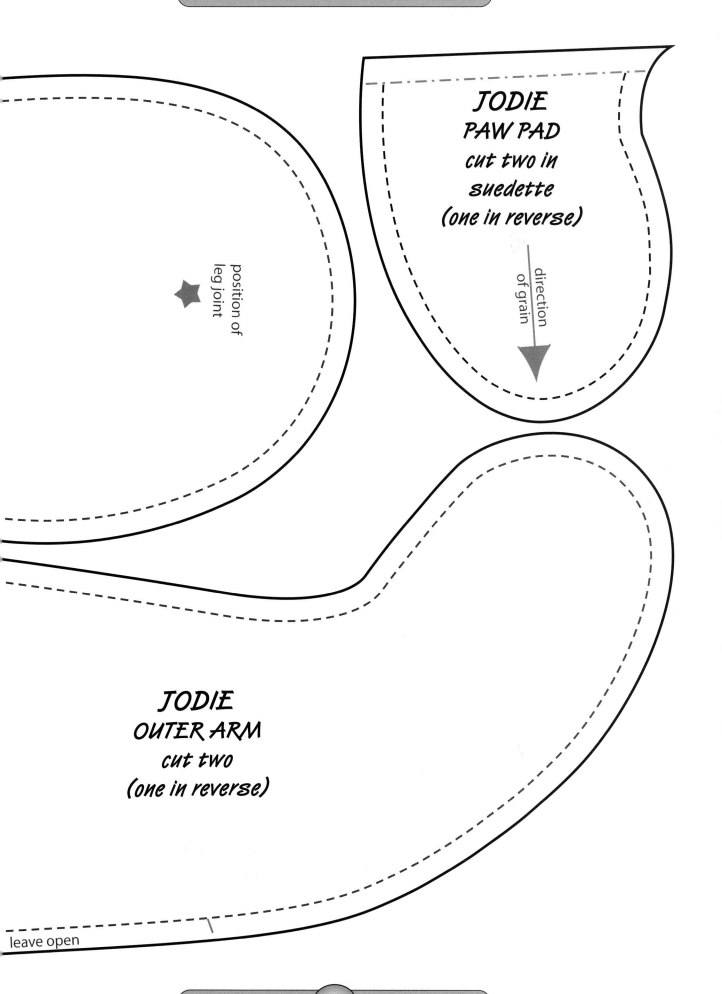

JODIE
PAW PAD
cut two in
suedette
(one in reverse)

direction
of grain

position of
leg joint

JODIE
OUTER ARM
cut two
(one in reverse)

leave open

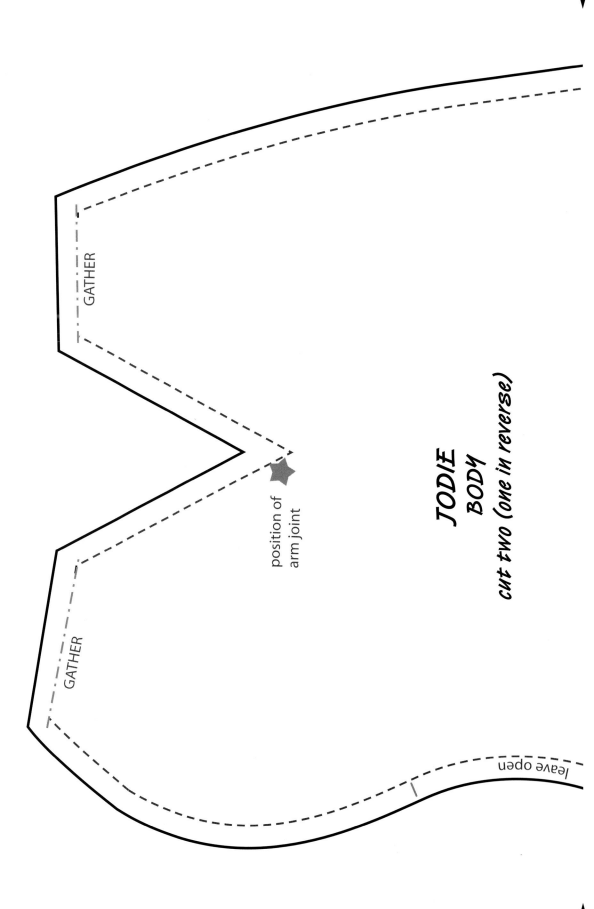

GATHER

GATHER

position of
arm joint

JODIE
BODY
cut two (one in reverse)

leave open

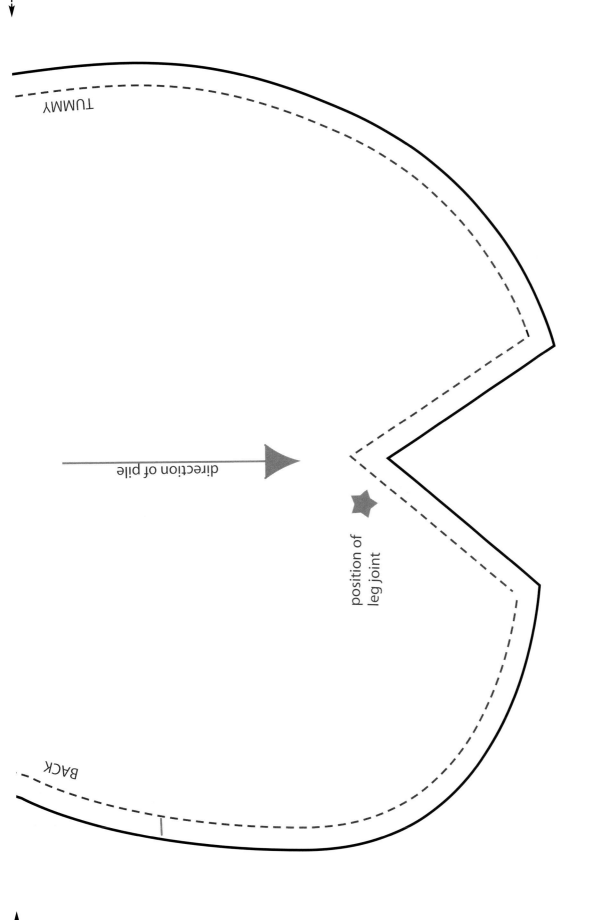

TUMMY

direction of pile

position of
leg joint

BACK

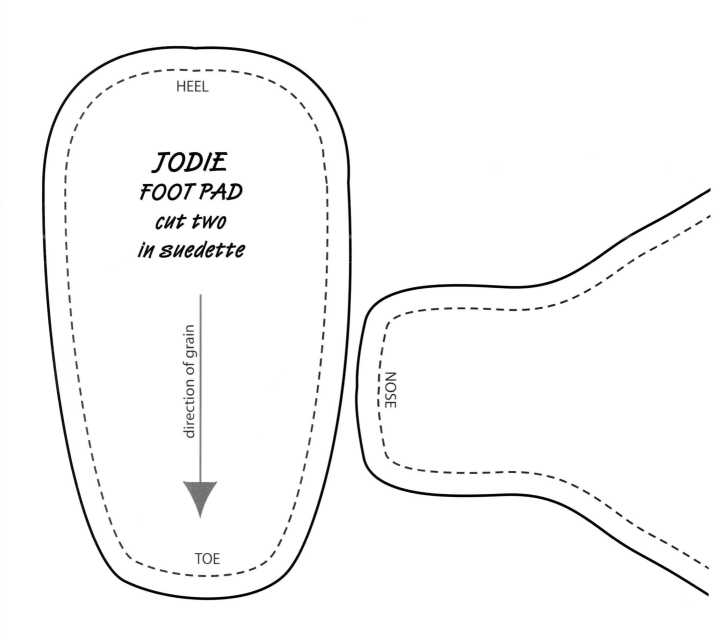

HEEL

JODIE
FOOT PAD
cut two
in suedette

direction of grain

TOE

NOSE

direction of pile

JODIE
HEAD GUSSET
cut one

NECK

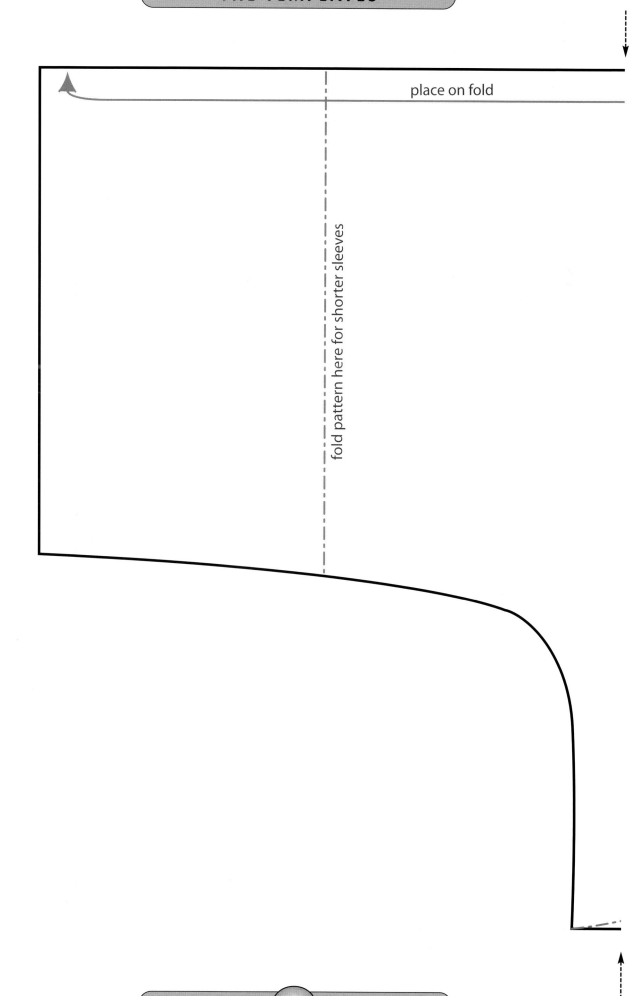

place on fold

fold pattern here for shorter sleeves

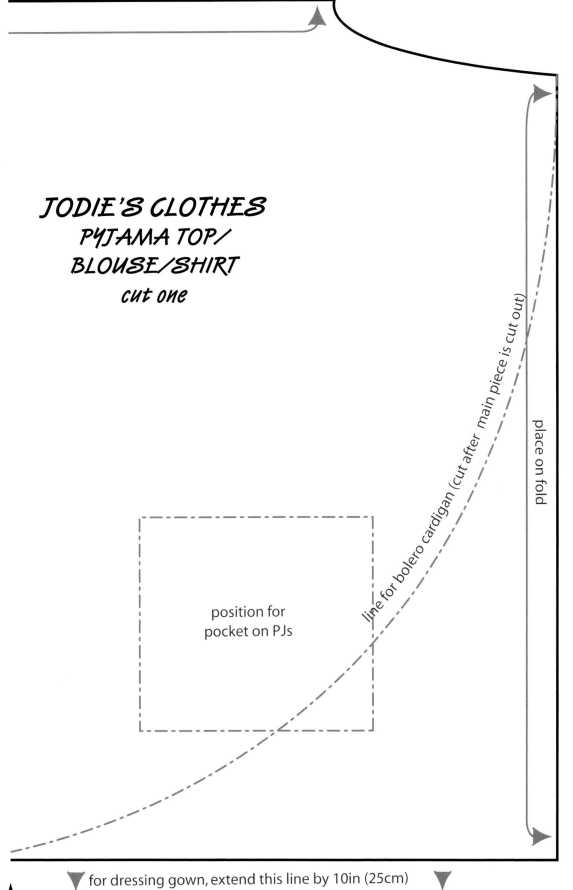

JODIE'S CLOTHES
PYJAMA TOP/ BLOUSE/SHIRT
cut one

place on fold

line for bolero cardigan (cut after main piece is cut out)

position for pocket on PJs

for dressing gown, extend this line by 10in (25cm)

place on fold

WAIST

centre back and centre front seams

JODIE'S CLOTHES
TROUSERS/SHORTS/PYJAMA BOTTOMS
cut two

fold pattern here for shorts

BOTTOM OF LEG

inside leg seam

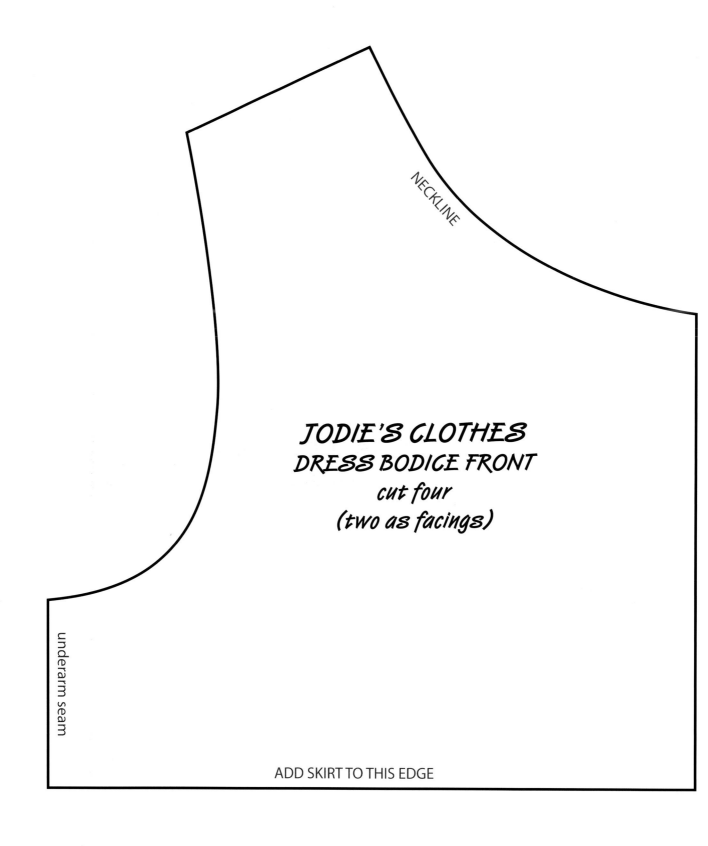

NECKLINE

JODIE'S CLOTHES
DRESS BODICE FRONT
cut four
(two as facings)

underarm seam

ADD SKIRT TO THIS EDGE

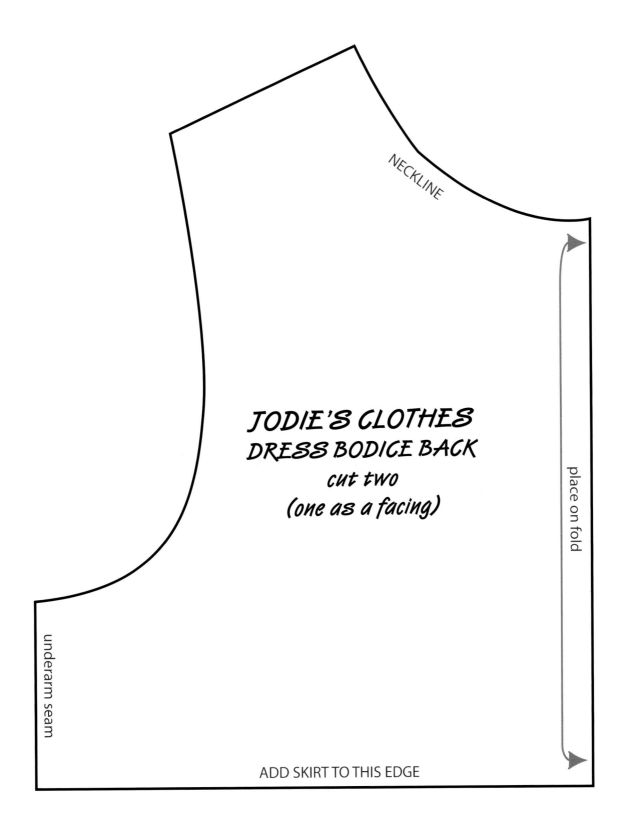

NECKLINE

JODIE'S CLOTHES
DRESS BODICE BACK
cut two
(one as a facing)

place on fold

underarm seam

ADD SKIRT TO THIS EDGE

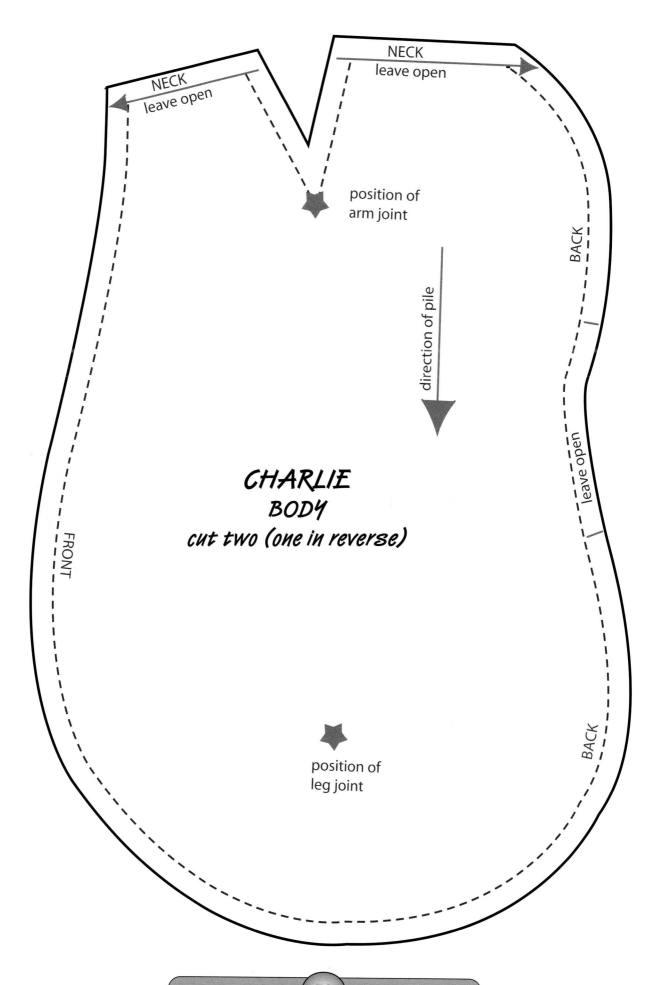

NECK
leave open

NECK
leave open

position of
arm joint

BACK

direction of pile

leave open

FRONT

CHARLIE
BODY
cut two (one in reverse)

BACK

position of
leg joint

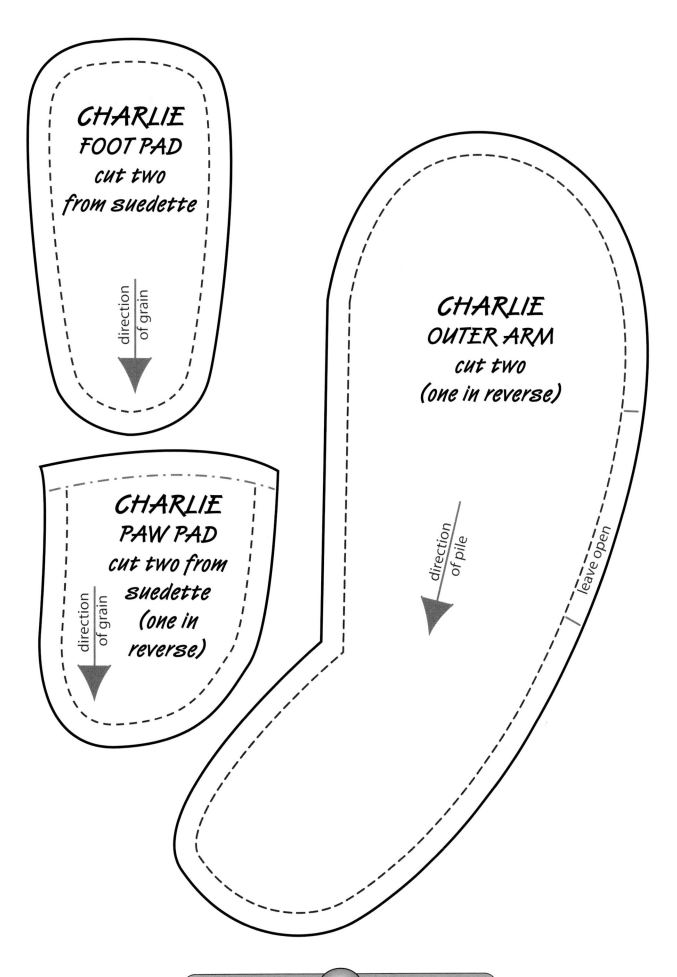

CHARLIE
FOOT PAD
cut two
from suedette

direction
of grain

CHARLIE
OUTER ARM
cut two
(one in reverse)

direction
of pile

leave open

CHARLIE
PAW PAD
cut two from
suedette
(one in
reverse)

direction
of grain

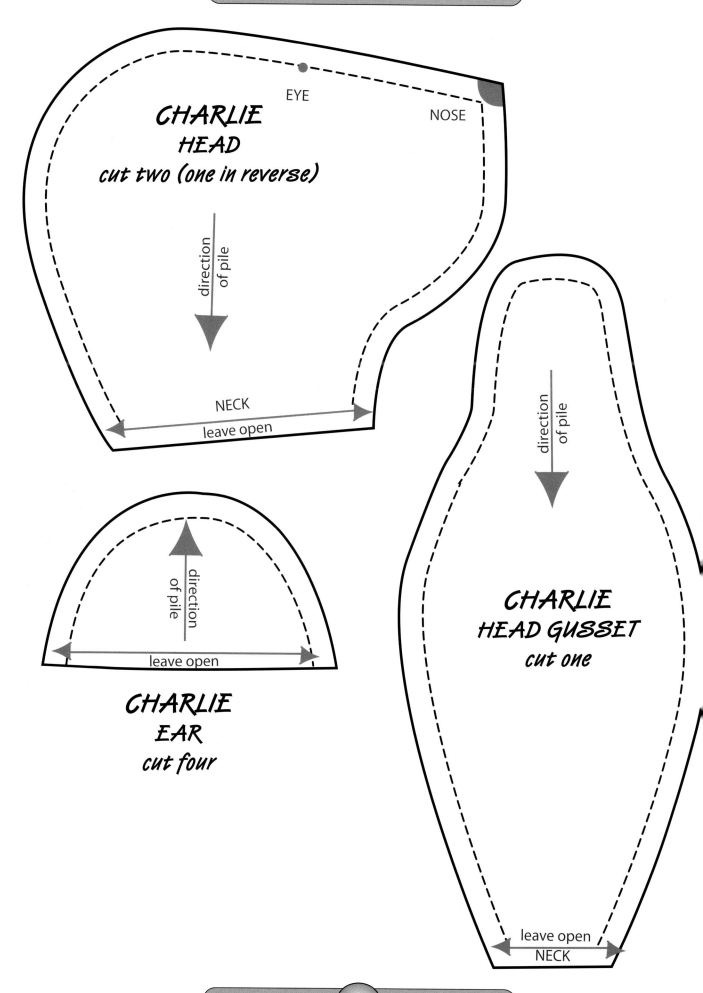

CHARLIE
HEAD
cut two (one in reverse)

EYE

NOSE

direction of pile

NECK
leave open

CHARLIE
HEAD GUSSET
cut one

direction of pile

CHARLIE
EAR
cut four

direction of pile

leave open

leave open
NECK

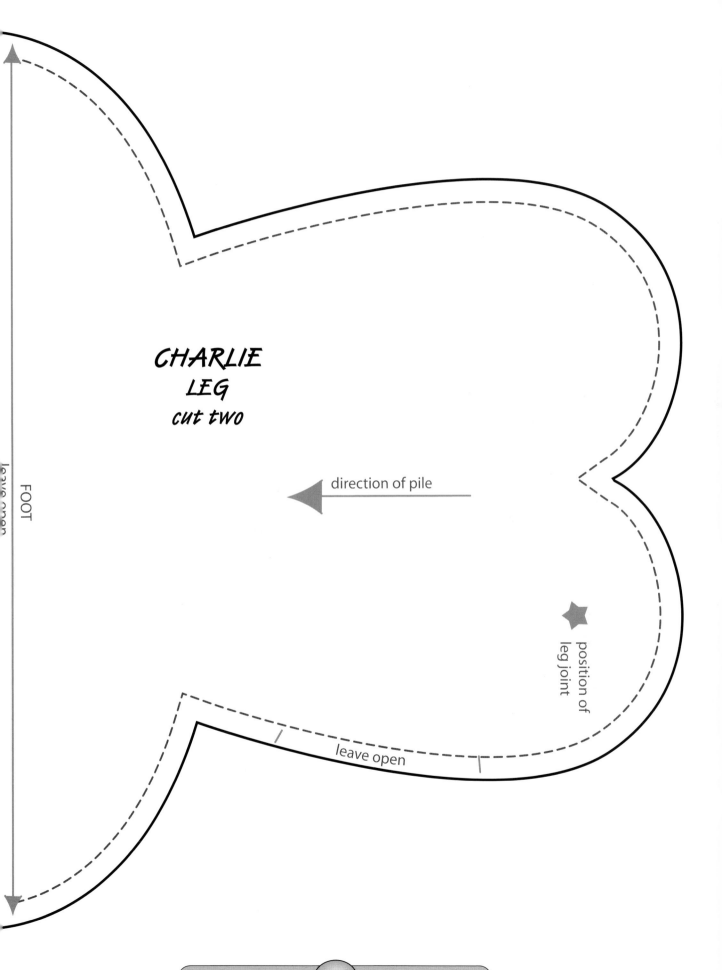

CHARLIE
LEG
cut two

direction of pile

position of
leg joint

FOOT

leave open

leave open

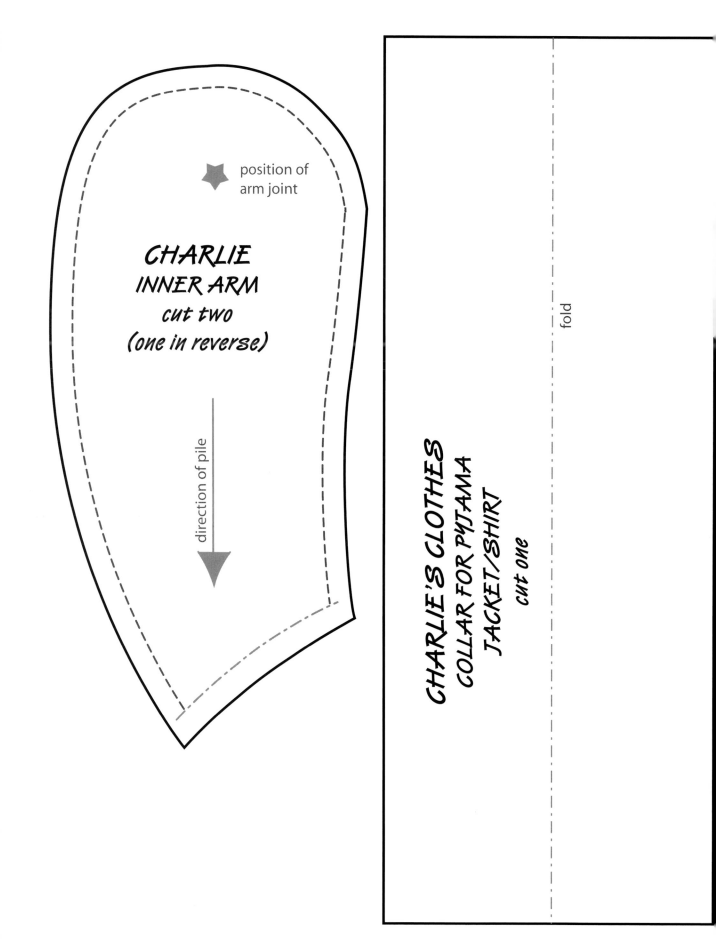

position of
arm joint

CHARLIE
INNER ARM
cut two
(one in reverse)

direction of pile

CHARLIE'S CLOTHES
COLLAR FOR PYJAMA
JACKET/SHIRT
cut one

fold

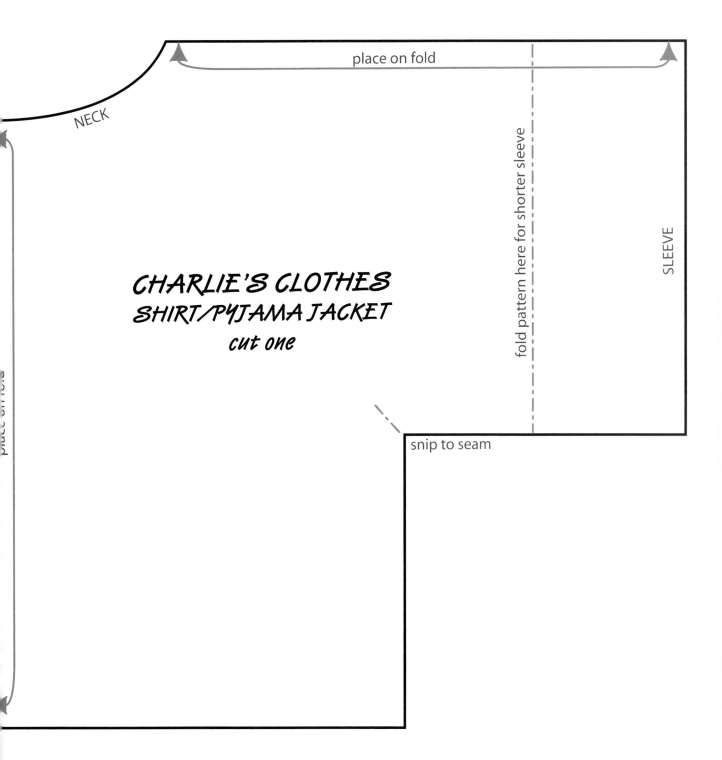

place on fold

NECK

fold pattern here for shorter sleeve

SLEEVE

CHARLIE'S CLOTHES
SHIRT/PYJAMA JACKET
cut one

snip to seam

WAIST

centre back and centre front seams

place on fold

CHARLIE'S CLOTHES
TROUSERS/SHORTS/
PYJAMA BOTTOMS
cut two

fold pattern here for shorts

inside leg seam

BOTTOM OF LEG

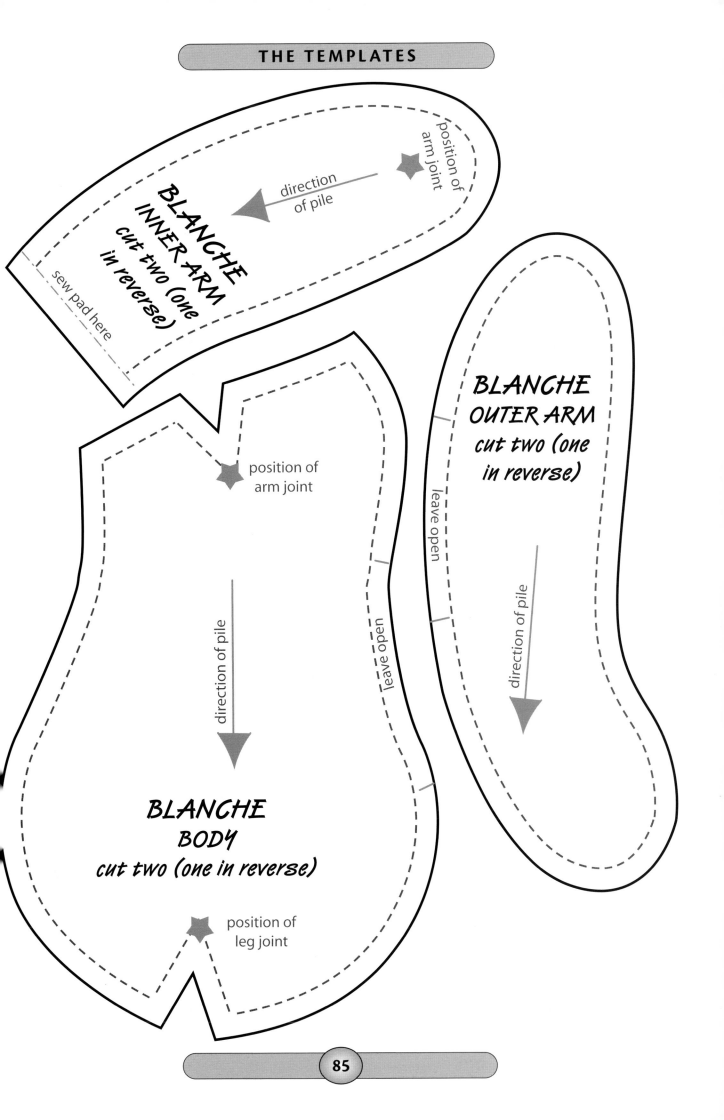

BLANCHE
INNER ARM
cut two (one
in reverse)

position of
arm joint

direction
of pile

sew pad here

position of
arm joint

BLANCHE
OUTER ARM
cut two (one
in reverse)

leave open

direction of pile

position of
arm joint

direction of pile

leave open

BLANCHE
BODY
cut two (one in reverse)

position of
leg joint

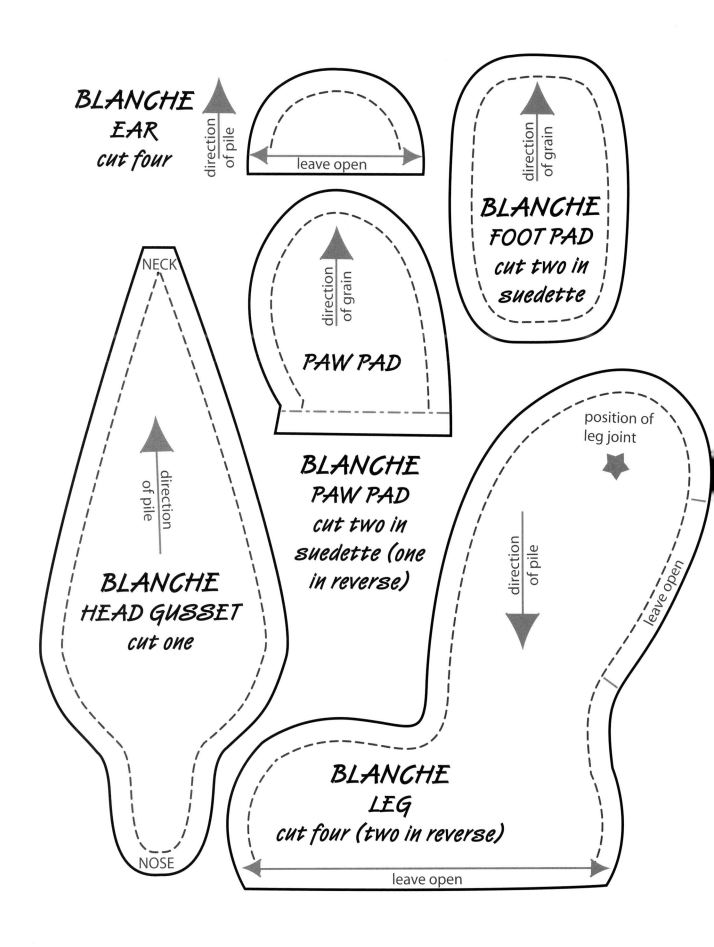

BLANCHE EAR cut four

direction of pile

leave open

BLANCHE FOOT PAD cut two in suedette

direction of grain

NECK

direction of pile

BLANCHE HEAD GUSSET cut one

NOSE

direction of grain

PAW PAD

BLANCHE PAW PAD cut two in suedette (one in reverse)

position of leg joint

direction of pile

leave open

BLANCHE LEG cut four (two in reverse)

leave open

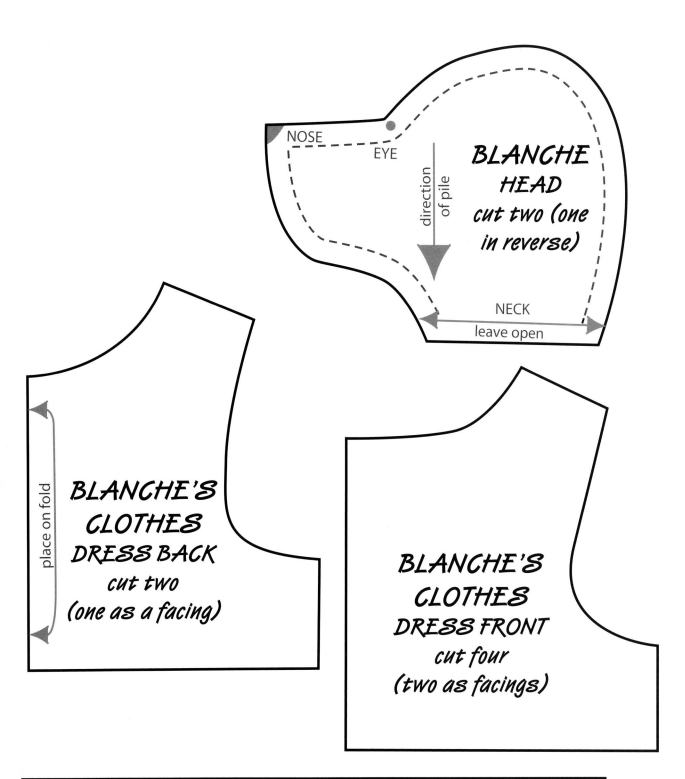

NOSE

EYE

direction of pile

BLANCHE HEAD
cut two (one in reverse)

NECK
leave open

place on fold

BLANCHE'S CLOTHES
DRESS BACK
cut two (one as a facing)

BLANCHE'S CLOTHES
DRESS FRONT
cut four (two as facings)

BLANCHE'S CLOTHES
COLLAR FOR PYJAMA JACKET AND BLOUSE
cut one

fold

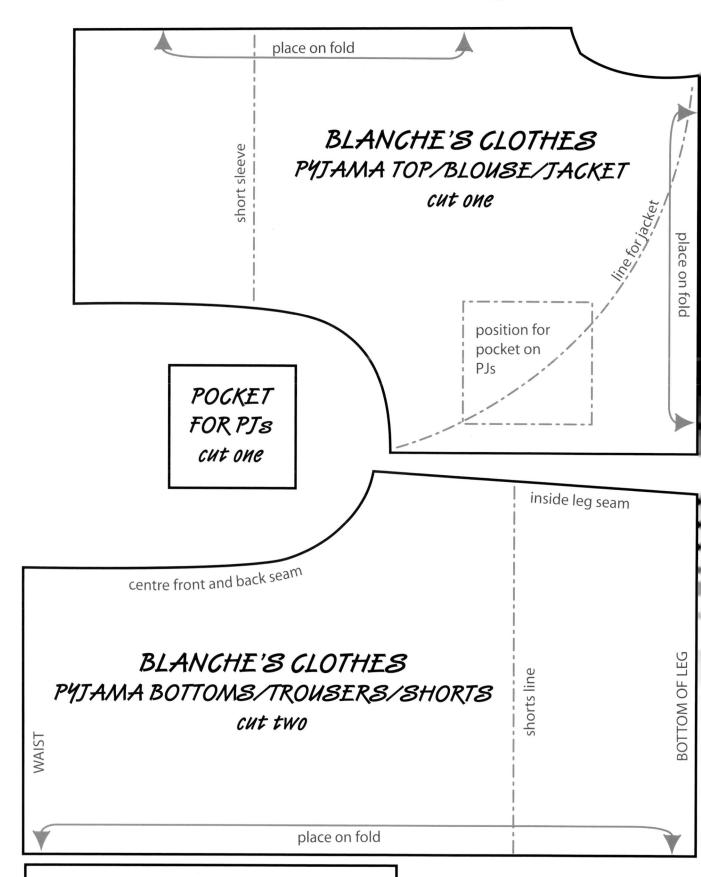

place on fold

short sleeve

BLANCHE'S CLOTHES
PYJAMA TOP/BLOUSE/JACKET
cut one

line for jacket

place on fold

position for pocket on PJs

POCKET FOR PJs
cut one

inside leg seam

centre front and back seam

BLANCHE'S CLOTHES
PYJAMA BOTTOMS/TROUSERS/SHORTS
cut two

shorts line

WAIST

BOTTOM OF LEG

place on fold

FACING FOR BLOUSE AND PYJAMA TOP
cut two

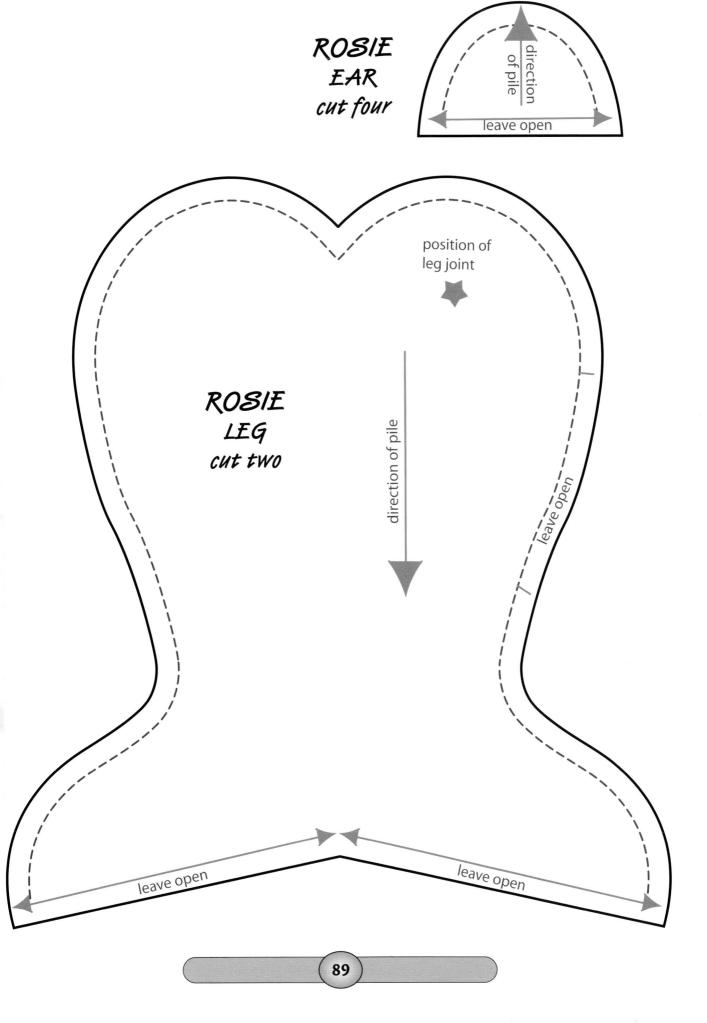

ROSIE
EAR
cut four

direction
of pile

leave open

ROSIE
LEG
cut two

position of
leg joint

direction of pile

leave open

leave open

leave open

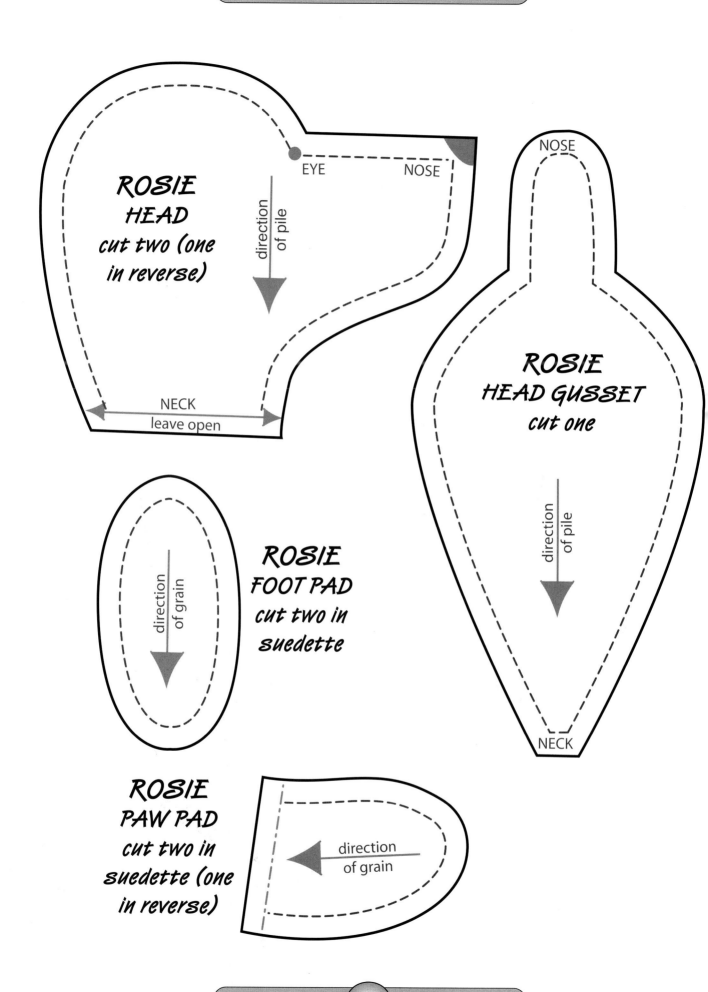

ROSIE HEAD
cut two (one in reverse)

EYE

NOSE

direction of pile

NECK
leave open

ROSIE HEAD GUSSET
cut one

NOSE

direction of pile

NECK

ROSIE FOOT PAD
cut two in suedette

direction of grain

ROSIE PAW PAD
cut two in suedette (one in reverse)

direction of grain

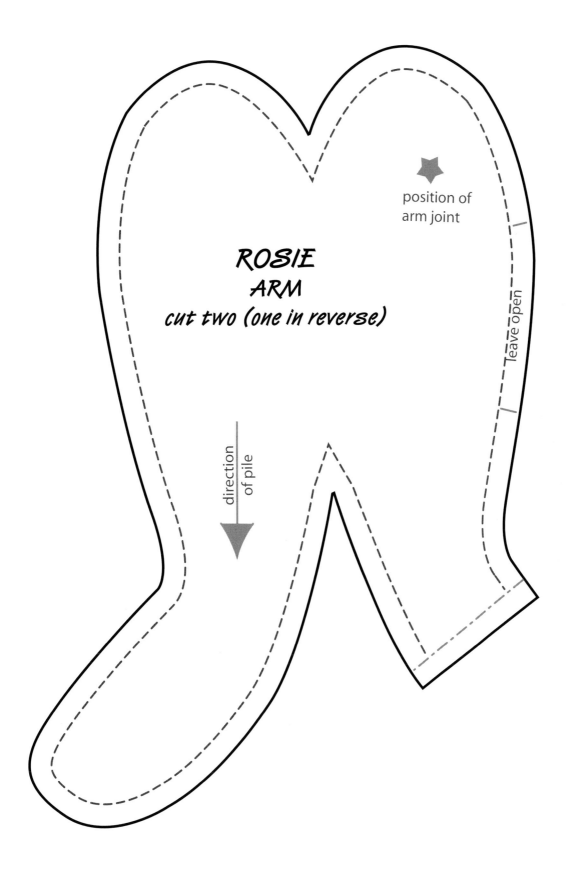

ROSIE
ARM
cut two (one in reverse)

position of
arm joint

leave open

direction
of pile

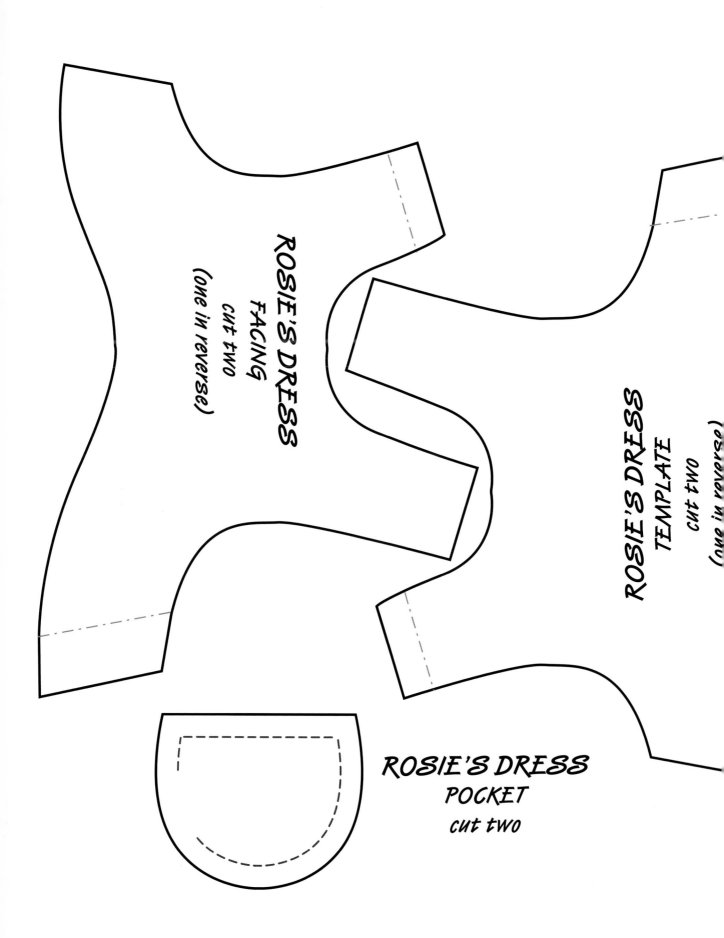

ROSIE'S DRESS
FACING
cut two
(one in reverse)

ROSIE'S DRESS
TEMPLATE
cut two
(one in reverse)

ROSIE'S DRESS
POCKET
cut two

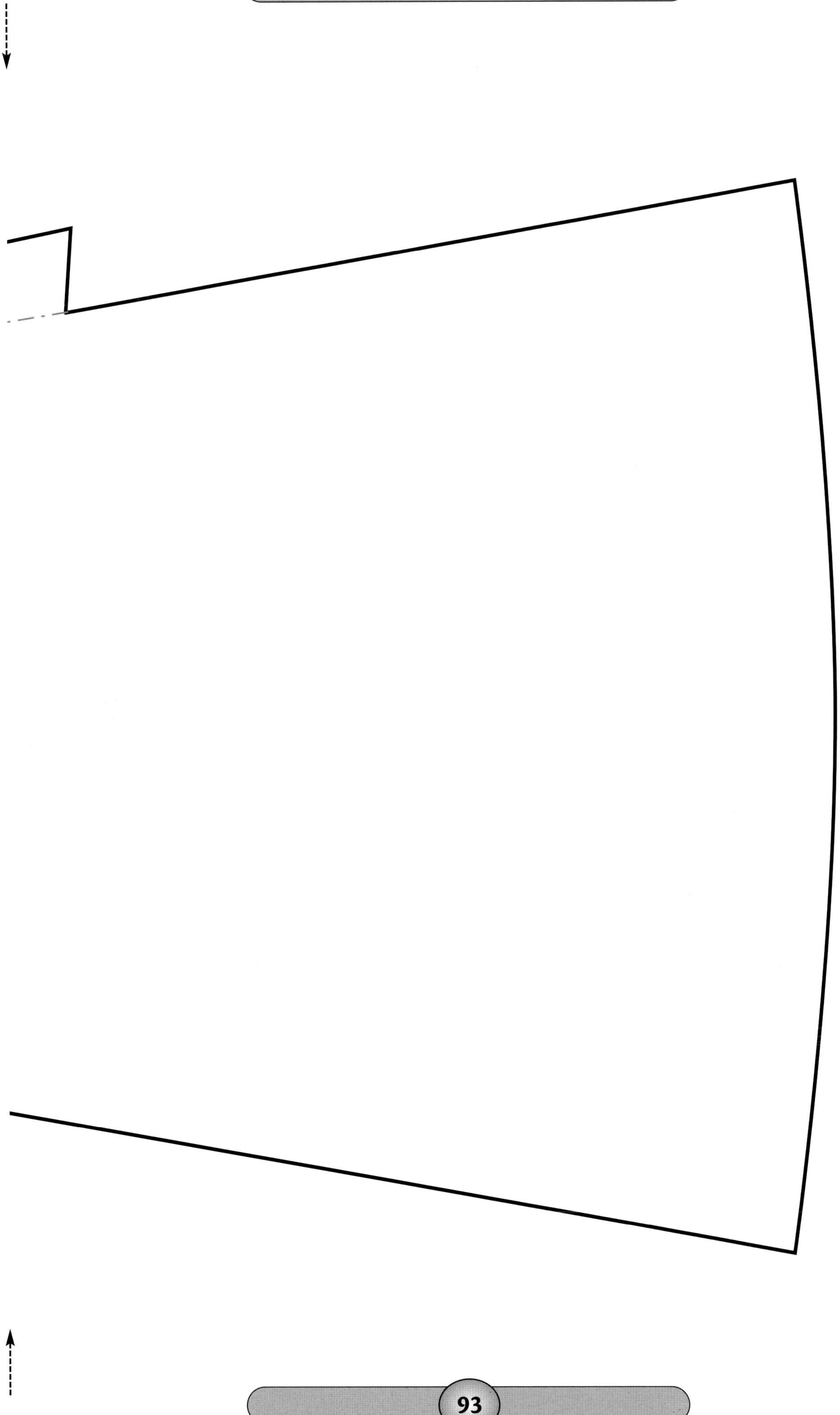

BLANCHE'S WHOLECLOTH QUILT

Theodore
1902~2002

Look out for these other titles in the

Craftworld Series

Quilting With A Difference
Nikki Tinkler

Are you a hand-quilter looking for a new twist to your work? In Quilting With A Difference Nikki shows you how to add visual interest to the surface of your work while you quilt, using traditional embroidery stitches. Each stitch is illustrated with clear step-by-step instructions for both right-handed and left-handed students, and a selection of easy-to-follow projects gives you a chance to try out your new-found skills.

144 PAGES, FULL COLOUR THROUGHOUT, A4 FORMAT, PAPERBACK   ISBN 1 900371 70 7

Log Cabin Landscapes
Dorothy Stapleton

Whether you're a complete beginner, or already familiar with the log cabin technique, this book will open your eyes to a whole world of possibilities! Dorothy's already well known for her log cabin houses; now she's gathered all these patterns together in one volume, and added all kinds of other landscapes and buildings too. The book is packed with full-colour photographs of Dorothy's stitched examples and the patterns for creating them, plus inspirational photographs from around the world.

120 PAGES, FULL COLOUR THROUGHOUT, A4 FORMAT, PAPERBACK   ISBN 1 900371 75 8

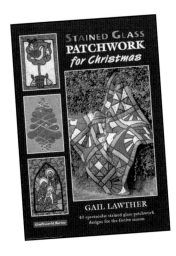

Stained Glass Patchwork for Christmas
Gail Lawther

Stained glass patchwork is the perfect technique for Christmas designs; it's bold, colourful, and easy to do! In this wonderful book Gail introduces the technique in detail and also gives designs for 40 spectacular projects to celebrate the festive season. Christmas trees and snowflakes, angels and stars, poinsettias and plum puddings; you'll find them all in the pages of this book, just waiting to be stitched on everything from simple tree decorations through to a full-size lap quilt. The book's packed with hints and tips, including advice on different bias bindings, and on using exotic fabrics such as silks, satins and metallics.

120 PAGES, A4 FORMAT, PAPERBACK   ISBN 1 900371 80 4

To purchase any of these titles, contact Traplet Publications Ltd via any of the following methods:

- *Write to* Traplet Publications Ltd, Traplet House, Severn Drive, Upton upon Severn, Worcs WR8 0JL, UK
- *Telephone* the Sales department on 01684 595300